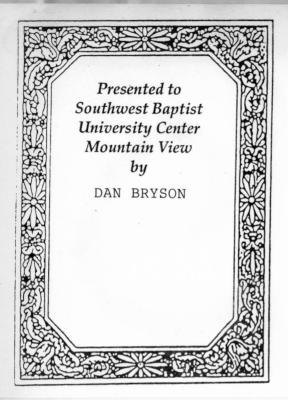

New Testament Evangelism

NEW TESTAMENT EVANGELISM

The Eternal Purpose

Herschel H. Hobbs

Convention Press

NASHVILLE   **TENNESSEE**

© 1960 • CONVENTION PRESS
Nashville, Tennessee

511-00107

Code Number: Church Study Course for
Teaching and Training
This book is number 0107 in Category 1,
Section A

Library of Congress Catalog Card Number: 60-14371
Printed in the United States of America
15. JUL 60 R.R.D.

About the Author

HERSCHEL H. HOBBS is a native of Alabama. He is a graduate of Howard College and the Southern Baptist Theological Seminary. At the latter institution he received the Th.M. and Ph.D. degrees. Howard College conferred upon him the D.D. degree in 1941. He is married to Frances Jackson Hobbs, and they have one son, Jerry.

Doctor Hobbs has held many positions of responsibility in Baptist life. He has served on the following boards of the Southern Baptist Convention: Foreign Mission Board, New Orleans Baptist Theological Seminary, and Oklahoma Baptist University Board of Trustees (president 1956-1957). At present he is a member of the Executive Committee of the Southern Baptist Convention, serving as chairman of its program committee.

He is a past president of the Southern Baptist Pastors' Conference and of the Baptist General Convention of Oklahoma. In 1958 he preached the sermon at the Southern Baptist Convention. Since October, 1958, he has been the preacher on the Baptist Hour. He is the author of ten other books and is a contributor to several others. His book *Studies in Hebrews* has been published in Portuguese.

Doctor Hobbs has held pastorates in Alabama, Kentucky, Indiana, and Oklahoma. From the Dauphin Way Baptist Church, Mobile, Alabama, he went to his present pastorate, First Baptist Church, Oklahoma City, Oklahoma.

In 1955, Doctor and Mrs. Hobbs toured Europe and the Middle East. In 1959 they made a missionary trip around the world, during which he held evangelistic meetings in Japan and Korea. He is constantly preaching at evangelistic conferences throughout the United States.

Contents

Church Study Course for Teaching and Training....... viii

Requirements for Credit in Class or Home Study....... ix

Introduction xi

1. THE NEW TESTAMENT CONCEPT...................... 1

2. THE REDEMPTIVE PURPOSE OF GOD................... 15

3. THE DIVINE AGENT............................... 31

4. THE HUMAN RESPONSE............................ 47

5. THE NEW TESTAMENT PRINCIPLES AND PATTERN
   (In the Ministry of Jesus)........................ 61

6. THE NEW TESTAMENT PRINCIPLES AND PATTERN
   (In the Witness of the Churches).................. 77

7. THE RELATION OF RELIGIOUS EDUCATION TO EVANGELISM. 91

8. THE INDIVIDUAL AND EVANGELISM...................107

Teaching Suggestions 124

Audio-Visual Aids 126

Questions for Review and Written Work...............129

Church Study Course for Teaching and Training

THE Church Study Course for Teaching and Training began October 1, 1959. It is a merger of three courses previously promoted by the Baptist Sunday School Board—the Sunday School Training Course, the Graded Training Union Study Course, and the Church Music Training Course.

The course is fully graded. The system of awards provides a series of five diplomas of twenty books each for Adults or Young People, one diploma of ten books for Young People, two diplomas of five books each for Intermediates, and two diplomas of five books each for Juniors. All book awards earned previously in the Sunday School Training Course, the Graded Training Union Study Course, and the Church Music Training Course may be transferred to the new course.

The course is comprehensive. The books are arranged in nineteen categories. The purpose of the course is to help Christians to grow in knowledge and conviction, to help them to grow toward maturity in Christian character and competence for service, to encourage them to participate worthily as workers in their churches, and to develop leaders for all phases of church life and work.

The Church Study Course for Teaching and Training is promoted by the Baptist Sunday School Board, 127 Ninth Avenue, North, Nashville, Tennessee, through its Sunday School, Training Union, Church Music, and Church Administration Departments and by the Sunday school, Training Union, and Church Music departments of the states affiliated with the Southern Baptist Convention. A complete description of the course and the system of awards may be found in the *Church Study Course for Teaching and Training* catalog which may be obtained without charge from any one of these departments.

A record of all awards earned should be maintained in each church. A person should be designated by the church to keep the files. Forms for such records may be ordered from any Baptist Book Store.

Requirements for credit for the study of this book may be found on page ix. This book provides credit in category 1, section A.

Requirements for Credit in Class or Home Study

IF CREDIT is desired for the study of this book in a class or by home study the following requirements must be met:

I. IN CLASSWORK

1. The class must meet a minimum of seven and one-half clock hours. The required time does not include assembly periods. Ten class periods of forty-five minutes each are recommended. (If laboratory or clinical work is desired in specialized or technical courses, this requirement may be met by six clock hours of classwork and three clock hours of supervised laboratory or clinical work.)

2. A class member who attends all class sessions and completes the reading of the book within a week following the last class session will not be required to do any written work.

3. A class member who is absent from one or more sessions must answer the questions on all chapters he misses. In such a case, he must turn in his paper within a week and he must certify that he has read the book.

4. The teacher should request an award for himself. A person who teaches a book in sections B, C, or D of any category or conducts an approved unit of instruction for Nursery, Beginner, or Primary children will be granted an award in category 11, Special Studies, which will count as an elective on his own diploma. He should specify in his request the name of the book taught, or the unit conducted for Nursery, Beginner, or Primary children.

5. The teacher should complete the "Request for Book Awards —Class Study" (Form 150) and forward it within two weeks after the completion of the class to the Church Study Course Awards Office, 127 Ninth Avenue, North, Nashville 3, Tennessee.

II. IN HOME STUDY

1. A person who does not attend any class session may receive credit by answering all questions for written work as indicated in the book. When a person turns in his paper on home study, he must certify that he has read the book.

2. Students may find profit in studying the text together, but

individual papers are required. Carbon copies or duplicates in any form cannot be accepted.

3. Home study work papers may be graded by the pastor or a person designated by him or they may be sent to the Church Study Course Awards Office for grading. The form entitled "Request for Book Awards—Home Study" (Form 151) must be used in requesting awards. It should be mailed to Church Study Course Awards Office, 127 Ninth Avenue, North, Nashville 3, Tennessee.

III. CREDIT FOR THIS BOOK

This book is number 0107 in category 1, section A.

Introduction

EVANGELISM is the focal point of interest in Christian endeavor. Concepts and methods may vary with different groups. But by whatever title it may be called, it involves the effort of churches to reach lost people for Christ. Unfortunately, for many this work is limited to winning, with little or no emphasis upon developing those who are won.

The purpose of this study is to determine the principles and patterns found in New Testament evangelism. This is not primarily a book on methods. Its design is to create a proper understanding and appreciation for the work of evangelism itself, and to show this relevancy for today. Other books are available for the training of individual soul-winners, and for presenting detailed procedures for corporate effort.

Evangelism, in the New Testament sense of the word, is indispensable in Southern Baptist churches. Without it they will dwindle away and die. To a people who avoid catechisms and other similar methods of reaching "unchurched" people, the choice is between a vital effort in evangelism and ceasing to exist altogether. What is more important, it is the choice between leading persons to him who is "the way, the truth, and the life," and of permitting them to go unchallenged into eternity, destined only for being everlastingly lost, which is the "second death" (Rev. 14:20).

Therefore, this little volume is sent forth with the prayer that it may call the Lord's people to, and strengthen them in, that which is "every Christian's job."

HERSCHEL H. HOBBS

CHAPTER 1 OUTLINE

I. A DEFINITION OF TERMS
1. The Verb Form
2. The Noun Form
3. The Title
4. Some Related Words

II. THE SCOPE OF NEW TESTAMENT EVANGELISM
1. An Erroneous Concept
2. The Broader Aspect

III. THE ELEMENTS OF NEW TESTAMENT EVANGELISM
1. The Universal Need
2. The Universal Provision
3. The Universal Condition
4. The Universal Invitation
5. The Universal Goal

1

The New Testament Concept

THE New Testament is the final authority for the faith and practice of New Testament churches. While the roots of God's full and complete revelation are found in the Old Testament, the New Testament is the fruit of which the Old is the root.

Furthermore, the primary theme of the New Testament is evangelism. Mark begins with the words, "The beginning of the gospel of Jesus Christ, the Son of God" (Mark 1:1). Thenceforth the New Testament proceeds to tell of God's redemptive work through Jesus Christ, the beginning of the spread of the gospel to all nations through the Holy Spirit, and the promise of final victory of the believers.

The purpose of this volume is to examine this theme which runs throughout the New Testament. The purpose of this chapter is to look at it in a general way before proceeding to a more detailed study. What is New Testament evangelism?

I. A DEFINITION OF TERMS

To comprehend this subject requires an understanding of some of the terms relating to it. This study is confined to those New Testament words which define the meaning and process of evangelism.

1. The Verb Form

The English verb "to evangelize" is simply a transliteration of the Greek verb *euaggelizo*. In the Septuagint, the Greek translation of the Old Testament, it means to bring good news

1

or to announce glad tidings. It might refer to any kind of good news, tidings regarding God's kindness, and, in particular, to the messianic blessings.

But in the New Testament it is used particularly to declare the message of the coming of the kingdom of God, the salvation offered in Christ, and matters pertaining to that salvation. In one form or another it occurs fifty-five times in the New Testament.

These usages are borne out in evidence from the Greek papyri, fragmentary records regarding the everyday life of the people in the general area and time of the writing of the New Testament. For instance, one example is the announcement of a victory one had gained over an opponent. Better still, and more directly related to the New Testament message, is the use of this verb in saying "full of joy brings her the annunciation of the marriage" (cf. John 3:28 ff.) [1]

In the New Testament this verb is variously translated. It means preach, preach the gospel, bring good tidings, show good tidings, bring glad tidings, declare, declare glad tidings, be preached, and preached by the gospel.

2. *The Noun Form*

From this verb comes the noun *euaggelion,* meaning good news or glad tidings. From this noun comes the word "evangel." In the New Testament this word appears seventy-seven times, and is usually translated with the English word "gospel." The word "gospel" itself comes from the Anglo-Saxon words "god spel" meaning good tidings. In the four Gospels it refers largely to the kingdom of God or to the Messiah, the King of the kingdom. But after the resurrection of Jesus it comprises the sum total of the message involved in the death and resurrection, his place at the right hand of

1. James Hope Moulton and George Milligan, *The Vocabulary of the Greek New Testament,* (Grand Rapids: Wm. B. Eerdmans Publishing Company, 1949), p. 259.

God, and his second coming in majesty and glory. These various uses may be summed up as the glad tidings of salvation in Christ or the preaching of the grace of God offered through Christ.

3. *The Title*

A title coming from this word is "evangelist." It is simply the transliteration of the Greek word *euaggelistes,* meaning a bringer of good tidings. In the New Testament it is the title applied to a special group of Christian workers who were not apostles (Acts 21:8; Eph. 4:11; 2 Tim. 4:5). Perhaps these were workers who developed in a given area the work begun by the apostles. In our present-day language they would correspond to district missionaries.

The term "evangelist" is sometimes used in Christian thought to refer to the writers of the four Gospels. But note that it is found also on a pagan inscription to refer to one who announced the oracles at the Greek shrine of Daphne. Wherever used in the New Testament it contains the idea of one who announces the glad tidings of salvation in Jesus Christ.

4. *Some Related Words*

In addition to these words there are others related to the practice of evangelism.

(1) *Preach.*—Basically it referred to the duty of a herald. He might proclaim the results of an athletic contest (cf. 1 Cor. 9:27), or announce certain public events. The principal use was to describe one who was the bearer of news from a king or some other public official. In it was contained the idea of formality, of gravity, and of an authority which must be obeyed.

So when this word entered the Christian vocabulary it was filled with meaning. It referred to the public proclamation of the gospel by John the Baptist, Jesus, the apostles, and others. Those who preached the gospel did so in the name of the King. They declared with gravity and formality his will which must be heard and heeded.

(2) *Teach.*—Of greater interest in this study is the word "teach." It is a less formal word than "preach." A teacher might hold discourse formally as he taught those gathered for that express purpose. Or such teaching might be done more informally. The teacher sometimes taught his pupils as they walked along. This was a method often used by Jesus, both with his disciples and with some person or persons whom he met by the wayside.

In the New Testament the word "teach," and its kindred ones, is rich in meaning. Although Jesus is often described as preaching, he is never referred to by the title of "preacher." But he is repeatedly called "Master" or "Teacher." John the Baptist, the apostles, and others in Christian groups who undertook to witness through the power of the Holy Spirit, were referred to as teachers.

(3) *Disciple.*—This word, meaning pupil, was the title most often given to the followers of Jesus. He himself emphasized the importance of teaching when in the Great Commission he said: "As you go *disciple* all nations, . . . *teaching* them . . ." (Matt. 28:19-20, author's translation and italics).

(4) *Write.*—One final word worthy of note in this connection is the word "write." It is found often in the New Testament with reference to evangelism. Note again that the writers of the four Gospels are called evangelists. They were evangelists writing the gospel record of Jesus' redemptive ministry to be read and followed through the ages. The Acts is the written account of evangelism in action. The Pauline epistles are one phase of the apostle's evangelistic work covering a great portion of the Roman world. The epistle to the Hebrews is a challenge to the first-century Christians to go forward in the fulfilment of their part in God's redemptive purpose. The Revelation is a written exhortation to fearless

effort in the cause of evangelism, with the promise of victory for those who were faithful in their calling.

So evangelism is the work of declaring formally the good news of the kingdom of God, of his salvation through Jesus Christ. It is also both formal and informal instruction with regard to the same good news. It is using the pen to that end.

II. The Scope of New Testament Evangelism

At the outset of this study it is important that the scope of New Testament evangelism be understood.

1. *An Erroneous Concept*

Unfortunately the most widely held concept of evangelism is an erroneous one. It involves only one aspect of the evangelistic process. The popular idea of evangelism is related only to the redemption of the soul, with little or no regard for the Christian life which follows.

In most minds the word "salvation" is limited to the initial experience of regeneration. A preacher once referred to the larger aspect of salvation. After the service a consecrated Sunday school teacher said: "I always thought of salvation as an instantaneous act. I thought that God did what he did immediately." He was thinking of the new birth which is an instantaneous act. But he spoke for legions of people. Salvation is that, but it is much more.

Many of the most hurtful errors in Christian thought and practice may be traced to this limited understanding of salvation.

(1) *Salvation by faith plus works.*—Thinking of salvation only in the sense of redemption, many seek to relate the New Testament teachings regarding conduct to the saving of the soul.

During World War II a famous American, upon being rescued from a lifeboat at sea, was asked if he was a Christian. He replied, "Yes, I try to live by the Golden Rule." But the Sermon on the Mount was not given as a means of redemption. It was intended to teach redeemed people how to live.

In a seminary class a professor asked a student to explain the passage "Work out your own salvation with fear and trembling. For it is God which worketh in you both to will and to do of his good pleasure" (Phil. 2:12-13). The student said, "It means working out what God has already worked in you." To which the professor replied, "I do not believe I could explain it any better than that."

(2) *Falling from grace.*—Believing that salvation, or redemption, is through faith in Christ's redeeming work plus a person's own good deeds, naturally leads many to conclude that the permanency of redemption depends upon that person's continuing in good works. Failing in this, redemption is lost altogether, thus making necessary another experience of grace.

A church once reported more than fifty conversions during a revival. Since this was an unusual number in that town, another pastor inquired as to the nature of these conversions. He was told that most of them were church members who had fallen from grace and were saved again.

Such a belief ignores the gospel of grace altogether. Only twice does the New Testament refer to falling from grace (Gal. 5:4; Heb. 12:15). In both instances it refers to one forsaking the grace way of redemption for one of law. In each case the meaning is not that of being in grace and then falling out of it. Rather the picture is that of a person repudiating the grace way of salvation for that of law, with the inescapable question as to whether he ever was "in grace."

When a certain preacher lay dying, he was asked: "What do you say now? How do you propose to be saved?" He replied: "My frail ship is about to put out to sea. Realizing that,

I am throwing overboard all of my cargo of good works. I propose to float to glory on the plank of free grace."

(3) *Wrong view of sanctification.*—In the belief that works are related to the initial experience of redemption, they find little or no place in the experience of sanctification. Thus this great teaching is removed from the area of the practical out-workings of the Christian life that is within. Instead it is thought of in terms of certain mystical and overly emotional experiences. It is regarded in a negative instead of a positive way. It is thought of as getting rid of sin rather than of em-ploying good works as a means of growing into the likeness of Jesus Christ.

A certain man once exclaimed, "I am as good as Jesus, and am getting better every day." If this sounds like blasphemy, take it rather as the outgrowth of an erroneous view of sancti-fication.

(4) *Weak, ineffective Christian lives.*—This is largely the case of those who regard salvation as one instantaneous ex-perience with little or no relation to the Christian living which follows.

Suppose that a baby was born but never grew. Or a child enrolled in school but never studied. In the physical and in-tellectual realms such cases are rare. But in the Christian life unfortunately this often happens. For that reason multi-tudes of Christian people are dwarfs, both spiritually and intellectually. The result is lives that are not only negative in their fruit bearing, they are positive in sinful living. Such a Christian has little concept of that which is expected of a redeemed child of God. The result is little expected, little attempted, little done!

(5) *Failure in the ministry of enlistment and develop-ment.*—Many churches do not recognize their responsibility beyond the initial act of winning the lost person to Christ. Consequently multitudes of unenlisted Christians do not even

hold membership in churches where they live. Myriads feel no sense of responsibility to be active in the churches where they hold membership. A pitiful few ever endeavor to win another person to Christ. These conditions will never be changed without a rethinking of the meaning of the word "salvation."

2. *The Broader Aspect*

The broader aspect of evangelism may be seen in a brief study of the word "salvation." It has many uses in the Bible.

In the Septuagint it is used to translate Hebrew words meaning to save, to keep safe, or to rescue from danger or destruction. In the New Testament it is used occasionally in these senses. Sometimes it speaks of healing, maybe physical, maybe spiritual (Matt. 9:22; Luke 7:50). But by far the greater use is with regard to one partaking of the salvation offered by Christ (Matt. 19:25; John 3:17). It is in this last sense that it is considered here.

In this light the word "salvation" is employed in three different ways. It speaks of redemption or the new birth (Eph. 2:8). It refers to growth in grace, knowledge, and service (2 Cor. 1:6; Phil. 2:12). It is used also to refer to arrival in heaven and beyond (Rom. 13:11; Heb. 9:28). Thus in the New Testament salvation is used to express an instantaneous act, a continuing process, and an ultimate experience. Instead of salvation being regarded as one element of the Christian experience, it covers the whole of it.

When a baby is born he has not reached the ultimate goal. He has just begun. When a person enrols in school he becomes a pupil, but the process of development has only started. When two people marry the wedding ceremony is not the end but the beginning. All of these figures, and others, are used in the New Testament to refer to the initial experience of becoming a Christian. Each entails a continuing process and an ultimate goal.

This is not to say that the soul is redeemed through a process. The regeneration of the soul occurs the moment that one believes in Christ. In that split second of time Satan loses the soul. But he endeavors to capture the life for his own nefarious ends. In so doing he gains other souls through the failure of the Christian's witness. And he makes meager indeed this Christian's present joy and future reward in heaven.

Thus in the following pages evangelism will be seen in its larger aspect, as instantaneous, continuing, and ultimate. These three experiences are also called, respectively, justification, sanctification, and glorification.

III. The Elements of New Testament Evangelism

A brief glance at the New Testament will reveal its emphasis upon the broader aspect of evangelism. Regarding the New Testament as basic in this regard, one cannot ignore its message without penalty personally or to others.

1. *The Universal Need*

In Romans 3:23 Paul affirms that "all have sinned, and come short of the glory of God." This verse is the climax of his reasoning to the effect that the entire human race stands guilty and condemned before God (Rom. 1 to 3.) This is true whether it be regarded in terms of the race or of individuals.

A mother said to her pastor about a ten-year-old child, "Of course, she has never done anything really bad." Perhaps not. But this did not mean that she was not lost.

What must a person do to be lost? He needs to stay only as he is, for he is lost already! Jesus said: "He that believeth on him [Christ] is not condemned: but he that believeth not is condemned already, because he hath not believed in the name of the only begotten Son of God" (John 3:18). And that is the teaching of all the New Testament.

Of course this must be understood in the light of the ability to make a personal choice. Until a child reaches the age of accountability, he is not held accountable for his condition. The age of accountability assumes a developed intelligence which is not found in infants or those of mental deficiency. The burden of New Testament teaching is that those who are mentally deficient or normal persons who die in infancy are saved by the grace of a merciful God in Christ Jesus. Bernard Ramm defines the age of accountability as "that invisible boundary a person crosses when he has matured to the point at which he can justly be held answerable for his conduct . . . . Individuals mature at different rates; some powers develop faster than others; thus no precise age of accountability may be specified."[2] The danger is evident in a failure to recognize that a child has reached such a place in his development. Those who work with children must be as wise as serpents and as harmless as doves.

2. *The Universal Provision*

The theme of the New Testament is that God has made provision for every person to be saved. In 2 Corinthians 5:18-19 Paul writes: "And all things are of God, who hath reconciled us to himself by Jesus Christ, and hath given to us the ministry of reconciliation; to wit, that God was in Christ, reconciling the world unto himself, not imputing their trespasses unto them; and hath committed unto us the word of reconciliation."

Thus God in Christ has made the provision for salvation. He has committed the gospel of salvation to his people. The rest is up to them!

Someone asked Charles H. Spurgeon if the heathen would be saved if Christian people did not preach the gospel to

2. *Encyclopedia of Southern Baptists,* I (Nashville: Broadman Press, 1958), 4.

them. His reply was: "The question is, are we saved if we do not preach the gospel to them?" It is a question to ponder.

3. *The Universal Condition*

In Ephesians Paul says: "For by grace are ye saved through faith; and that not of yourselves: it is the gift of God: not of works, lest any man should boast" (Eph. 2:8-9). Analyzed, here is what Paul is saying. Salvation, in the sense of redemption, is a gift of the grace of God offered through Jesus Christ. The lost man appropriates it unto himself by means of faith in Jesus Christ. He cannot save himself by his good works. It is a gift which he must receive.

This is the condition placed by a sovereign God. It is one which every man, woman, and child can meet.

One of the most vicious attitudes is that which says that it does not matter what a man believes so long as he is sincere in his belief. This attitude is not consistent with life. It would not be tolerated in pharmacy, surgery, mathematics, or in any other phase of life. It should be much less tolerated in matters of the soul.

The New Testament certainly does not teach this attitude. Its message is typified by Paul: "But though we, or an angel from heaven, preach any other gospel unto you than that which we have preached unto you, let him be accursed" (Gal. 1:8). Strong language! But not too strong where the salvation of immortal souls is concerned.

4. *The Universal Invitation*

Near the close of the book of Revelation are these words: "And the Spirit [Holy Spirit] and the bride [church] say, Come. And let him that heareth [Christian] say, Come. And let him that is athirst [lost person] come. And whosoever will [is willing], let him take the water of life freely" (22:17).

This is the theme of the Bible. It is a fitting finale to God's written revelation of his will and purpose. It is a challenge to every segment of the Christian body. It is God's last invitation to a lost world!

Dr. George W. Truett said: "A church that is not missonary does not deserve the ground upon which its building stands. For 'the earth is the Lord's, and the fulness thereof; the world, and they that dwell therein'" (Psalm 24:1). Missions is evangelism, and evangelism is missions.

5. *The Universal Goal*

"And he gave some, apostles; and some, prophets; and some, evangelists; and some, pastors and teachers; for the perfecting of the saints, for the work of the ministry, for the edifying of the body of Christ: till we all come in [into] the unity of the faith, and of the knowledge of the Son of God, unto a perfect [complete] man, unto the measure of the stature of the fulness of Christ: that we henceforth be no more children, tossed to and fro, and carried about with every wind of doctrine, by the sleight of men, and cunning craftiness, whereby they lie in wait to deceive; but speaking the truth in love, may grow up into him in all things, which is the head, even Christ" (Eph. 4:11-15).

The former passage includes the total depravity of unredeemed human nature (Eph. 2:1-3). It pictures the mercy and love of God (2:4). Here Christ is seen as the incarnation of God and as the instrument of his grace (2:5). It further reveals the ultimate purpose of Christ's redemptive work (2:6-7). The proper relationship between grace and works is set forth: the former is the means of redemption; the latter is the means of Christian development (2:8-10).

The latter reference lists the human instruments through which God completes the salvation which begins with redemption and reaches unto complete sanctification (4:11). It depicts the growth and development of the redeemed individually and collectively into a Christian body in keeping with Christ, the Head of the body (4:12-15). Evangelism which proposes to do less falls short of the New Testament ideal.

FOR DISCUSSION AND CLASSWORK

1. What is meant by saying that the Bible is the inspired Word of God? Is the Old Testament inspired in the same way as the New Testament?
2. Why is it so important that evangelism be patterned after the New Testament? Could wise men today improve upon this pattern? Are churches ever justified in forsaking the New Testament pattern for some other?
3. Many Scripture verses have been cited in this chapter. Let each class member take certain ones, read them, and give his interpretation of them. Discuss these interpretations.

CHAPTER 2 OUTLINE

I. THE DIVINE WILL
    1. The Eternal Purpose
    2. The Eternal Aspect
    3. The Old Testament Revelation
    4. The New Testament Fulfilment

II. THE DIVINE PLAN
    1. The Doctrine of Election
    2. The Analysis of Election

III. THE DIVINE PROCEDURE
    1. The Divine Expectation
    2. The Divine Commission
    3. The Divine Example

2

The Redemptive Purpose of God

THE redemptive purpose of God is the central theme of the New Testament. And evangelism is the comprehensive method whereby that purpose may be achieved. The redemptive will of God is progressively revealed in the Bible. This is due not to God's inability to reveal, but to man's weakness to receive and comprehend that revelation. Thus God's purpose of redemption is more clearly set forth in John than in Genesis, in Ephesians than in Exodus, in Hebrews than in Leviticus, and in Romans than in Isaiah.

God's redemptive purpose is examined under three headings.

I. THE DIVINE WILL

The divine will expresses that which God wishes to do. Furthermore, it involves the work of God in bringing that wish to fruition. God's will and work center in his purpose to redeem all men.

1. The Eternal Purpose

In Ephesians 3:11 Paul refers to "the eternal purpose which he purposed in Christ Jesus our Lord." Literally Paul speaks of "the purpose of the ages," or of that which was in the heart of God before the creation of the world. The word "purpose" means that which is placed before. Even before the creation of man, an all-wise God knew that man would sin and be lost from him. And since God is righteous love,

15

he willed in eternity that his purpose was to save man from his sin.

Furthermore, he set in motion that which was necessary for man's redemption. This is seen in the verb "purposed." It means to carry into effect. So this purpose which was in the heart of the Eternal was carried into effect through Jesus Christ our Lord in the arena of history.

The work of evangelism, whether from the pulpit, in a classroom, or in some casual or purposeful visit in the name of the Lord, may seem for the moment to be an isolated event. But actually it is part and parcel of an eternal plan. It is God's timeless purpose to redeem lost people.

2. *The Eternal Aspect*

However, this carrying into effect of God's redemptive purpose is not confined to time. It is eternal also. This is seen in the words "the Lamb slain from the foundation of the world" (Rev. 13:8; cf. Matt. 13:35; 25:34; Eph. 1:4; Heb. 4:3). Thus the crucifixion was but the expression in time of that which had already occurred in eternity.

In Revelation 5 is pictured a book or roll perfectly sealed with seven seals. This has been variously called the book of justice, of God's eternal counsels or foreordained purposes, and the book of destiny. The author prefers to call it the roll of history from eternity to eternity. In symbolized form it declares God's dealings with the nations or with all men.

John wept because no man was worthy to unseal the roll. To unseal it suggests the revelation of the meaning of its contents. But "the Lion of the tribe of Juda, the Root of David, hath prevailed to open the book, and to loose the seven seals thereof" (Rev. 5:5). The scene is climaxed as the hosts of heaven fall down before the Lamb in praise as they sing: "Thou art worthy to take the book, and to open the seals thereof: for thou wast slain, and hast redeemed us to God by thy blood out of every kindred, and tongue, and people, and nation" (Rev. 5:9). The substance of this seems to be that only in the redemptive purpose of God in Christ is to be found the true interpretation of history.

Across the headlines of the daily press are emblazoned the stories of crime, death on the highways, political maneuvering, and other items of passing interest. But none of these ever makes the headlines of heaven. The announcement of an evangelistic service may be buried in some obscure place in the newspaper. A visit by a Sunday school teacher to the home of a lost child receives no notice at all. When that child makes a profession of faith in Christ it is not considered as being newsworthy. But "joy shall be in heaven over one sinner that repenteth, . . ." (Luke 15:7).

How vital these unheralded events are if only the long look were taken! In the middle thirties the headlines of the newspapers screamed of robberies and murders committed by John Dillinger. But almost lost in the accounts was the story of the same man when he was a teen-aged Sunday school boy. He had been enrolled in a Sunday school class. But one Sunday he was absent. These absences continued, and finally blended into a life of crime ended only by the guns of the FBI. Did the Sunday school teacher visit this absentee? Did he make any effort to win John Dillinger to Christ? Had he done so, and succeeded, the event would have received no notice in the daily press. But it would have received the acclaim of heaven. And of earth also, if men could have read the future.

Yes, the purpose of God in history is discovered in the witness of churches, or even of one individual, to the work of God.

3. *The Old Testament Revelation*

This eternal purpose is unfolded in time. Beginning dimly in the Old Testament, it reaches a crescendo of glory in the New Testament. Without presuming to deal at length with this gradual unveiling, note only its highlights. God's redemptive purpose may be seen as it emerges through the clouds which hover about the history of men and nations.

(1) *The Protevangelium.*—Within the very shadows of the gates of Eden God pronounced his judgment upon man's sin. But his justice was tempered with mercy as he gave what is known as the *Protevangelium.* "And I will put enmity between thee [serpent] and the woman, and between thy seed and her seed [Jesus Christ]; it shall bruise [crush] thy head, and thou shalt bruise [strike at] his heel" (Gen. 3:15). Many see in this conflict between Christ and Satan, with Christ being victorious. It is the "gospel" before the Gospels.

A father punishes his child for some act of disobedience. But even while he inflicts the penalty, he speaks words of endearment and love. That is but a finite picture of the infinite God (Psalm 103:8).

(2) *The system of sacrifice.*—The system of animal sacrifice in the Old Testament is but "a shadow of good things to come" (Heb. 10:1; cf. Gen. 3:21-22). The elaborate system of sacrifice under the Mosaic code is a foregleam of the sacrifice of Jesus (cf. Ex. 30:10; Num. 28:3). The author of Hebrews regards the death of Jesus as the fulfilment of all these (Heb. 9:11-14).

A Jewish rabbi remarked that the Jews have not practiced animal sacrifice for almost two thousand years. He did so not realizing that he had spoken the basic truth of the Christian gospel.

(3) *The prophetic portrayal.*—In prophetic utterance the Old Testament looks beyond this system of sacrifice to God's Suffering Servant (Isa. 42:1 ff.) through whom redemption will be offered to all people. Psalm 22 is a portrayal of Calvary almost a thousand years before the event. Isaiah 53 has been called the "Good Friday" of the Old Testament.

It is not surprising, therefore, to read Jesus' own words: "All things must be fulfilled, which were written in the law of Moses, and in the prophets, and in the psalms, concerning me. . . . Thus it is written, and thus it behooved Christ to suffer, and to rise from the dead the third day" (Luke 24: 44-46).

Suppose an announcement should appear in the newspaper that a great drama is to be presented. For ages the people have longed to see it. Finally the hour arrives. The audience is gathered and expectant. The curtain is raised. The prologue is presented. Then suddenly the curtain drops, and an announcement is made that that is all. The audience sits stunned with disappointment.

But that disappointment is as nothing compared to what that of the human race would have been had God's redemptive story ended with the last verse of Malachi. Someone has said that if one should read the New Testament without a knowledge of the Old Testament, he would ask, "Where is that which came before this?" If he should read the Old Testament without knowing about the New Testament, he would inquire, "But where is the rest of the story?" The New Testament completes that which the Old Testament began.

4. The New Testament Fulfilment

This may be seen in six brief affirmations.

(1) The eternal entered time.—In John 1:1-14 is the most eloquent statement of this truth. "In the beginning was the Word, and the Word was with God, and the Word was God [himself]." Here is the eternity of Christ, the equality of Christ with God, and the fact that Christ is God himself. And this eternal Word became flesh, and dwelt for a little while among men (John 1:14; Heb. 10:5-10). In him was grace and truth for all who would receive him (John 1:12, 14). This glorious truth is summarized in the "little gospel" (John 3:16).

A man listened to the Baptist Hour over the radio. The

preacher's message was a simple presentation of the plan of salvation. After the broadcast the man wrote that he was happier than he had ever been before in his life. For the first time he had heard that such a salvation was offered to him. The tragedy is that more in this world have not heard than have done so. A preacher once said that he spent very little time trying to figure out when Jesus is coming again. "So many people," said he, "have never heard that he came the first time!"

(2) *The divine demand justified.*—Was God justified in saying that all have sinned and come short of his glory (Rom. 3:23)? Is it possible for man to live in perfect accord with God's will? The answers are found in the life of Jesus. He "was in all points tempted like as we are, yet without sin" (Heb. 4:15).

This verse creates a problem for some. The author wrote the textbook *Studies in Hebrews.* In dealing with this verse he stated that Jesus had the capacity to sin, but did not do so. One day a friend reported that quite a discussion took place in one study group. The teacher took the position that Jesus could not sin. But in his effort to defend Jesus in this regard, he accused him of the sin of hypocrisy, a sin which Jesus condemned more than any other. (A "hypocrite" in Greek drama was one who played a part other than what he really was.)

In his life Jesus endured every kind of temptation. This is the meaning of Luke 4:13: "And when the devil had ended all the temptation, he departed from him for a season." Doctor A. T. Robertson comments: "These three kinds exhaust the avenues of approach (the appetites, the nerves, the ambitions). Satan tried them all." [1] One purpose of Jesus' various temptations was to demonstrate that it was possible for a human being to live in perfect accord with God's will. If it

1. A. T. Robertson, *Word Pictures in the New Testament* (Nashville: Baptist Sunday School Board, 1930), pp. 52-53.

were impossible for Jesus to do otherwise, his temptations were not real. He played a part which was a sham. The teacher of the textbook on Hebrews would not so claim.

No, the truth of the matter is that Jesus could sin. But the more glorious truth is that he did not sin. And in so doing he justified the divine demand for righteousness which God lays upon every man.

(3) *The demands of holiness met.*—A holy God could not ignore man's sin. Nor could a merciful God be indifferent to man's lost condition. Thus God was in a dilemma. How could he resolve this conflict within his nature? This he did when he condemned sin in the person of his beloved Son in whom he was well pleased.

The apostle Paul affirms this: "For he hath made him to be sin for us, who knew no sin; that we might be made the righteousness of God in him" (2 Cor. 5:21). The word "knew" means to know by personal experience. Though Jesus did not know sin in a personal experience of yielding to temptation, yet God made him to be sin, that in him he might condemn sin in the flesh.

At Calvary God did two things. He was "just" in that he punished sin in the person of Jesus. He became the "justifier" in that he offered justification to all who believe in Jesus (Rom. 3:26).

Billy Graham was stopped on one occasion for a minor traffic violation. When he appeared before the judge, the judge recognized him. Having levied a fine he paid it himself. Billy Graham said that this illustrated in a small way what God had done for him to an infinite degree. The judge did not ignore the law nor its violation. But having pronounced sentence, he took the sentence upon himself. The violator was allowed to go free, not because he was innocent, but because another had satisfied the just demands of a legal society for him.

This Jesus did when in his death he met the demands of

a holy God. Because he was bound we are free. Through his death we have life. As someone said, "Jesus became everything that we are that we might become everything that he is."

(4) *The divine love expressed.*—The crucifixion of Jesus was not the execution of a criminal, the death of a martyr, or a divine example. It was the expression of a divine love. For "God was in Christ, reconciling the world unto himself" (2 Cor. 5:19).

It is impossible to understand the redemptive purpose apart from God's love. Herein is the divine reason back of the creation of man. God, who is a person, could find a perfect expression of his love only as he bestowed it upon another person. Therefore God made man. He made him in his own image and for his fellowship. But sin marred both the image and the fellowship. The redemptive story is the work of a loving God as he sought to bridge the chasm created by sin.

In the restoration of fellowship the approach must be made by one of the parties involved. And since man by his sinful nature was in rebellion against God, the approach had to be made by God. This truth is affirmed in 1 John 4:8-10.

Thus in the crucifixion God destroyed the power of sin, that which hindered the free expression of love between God and man. This expression of God's love was designed to bring forth a like expression in man.

Two men, strangers to each other and each unaware of the other's presence, stood gazing at a painting of the crucifixion. Finally one of them whispered, "I love him!" Unconsciously the other added, "I love him too!"

(5) *The divine power triumphant.*—It is impossible to separate the cross from the empty tomb. On the cross God entered into mortal combat with Satan. In the resurrection he fully triumphed over Satan, as he declared Jesus to be the Son of God with power (Rom. 1:4). The word "declared" means

horizoned. After the darkness of the night of Calvary, the day of God's grace dawned to reveal the triumphant Son of God horizoned against the light of God's great salvation.

(6) *The divine grace offered.*—In Ephesians 4:8 Paul quotes Psalm 68:18 as being fulfilled in Jesus. "When he ascended up on high, he led captivity captive, and gave gifts unto men." This is the picture of the triumphal procession of a victorious general or king. The victor led his captives behind his chariot. From the booty of war he distributed gifts.

Jesus Christ entered heaven in a triumphal procession, leading the forces of evil behind his chariot. He made open show of his victory. Furthermore, he distributed gifts to men.

In Ephesians 4:11 Paul specified these gifts as apostles, prophets, evangelists, pastors, and teachers. And for what purpose? That he might through them offer his grace to all men; that those won to him might be developed in the faith; that they, in turn might become evangels of God's grace. This is evangelism in its entirety.

II. THE DIVINE PLAN

For the purpose of effecting his divine will God has a plan whereby his redemptive work may be offered to all men.

1. *The Doctrine of Election*

Central in this plan is the doctrine of election. Unfortunately this teaching is often confused in men's minds, and subsequently is neglected in both teaching and practice. To some it refers to a sovereign act of God whereby only certain individuals are elected to be saved while all others are elected to be lost. This attitude emphasizes the sovereign will of God to the neglect of the free will of man. Furthermore, it magnifies God's will and power, and minimizes his righteousness and love. The result is an attitude of fatalism.

This attitude is devastating in the area of evangelism. If some men are elected to salvation, and others are elected to damnation, with no consideration of man's free choice, why try to evangelize them at all? Furthermore, why should individuals be concerned about their personal salvation, if it has already been predetermined by a sovereign God?

To understand the doctrine of election one must consider both the sovereignty of God and the free will of man. In our finite minds they do not harmonize, but in the infinite mind of God they do.

Imagine two seemingly parallel perpendicular lines. Actually they come together one thousandth of an inch every one thousand miles. To the natural eye they are parallel. But somewhere in outer space they intersect. So to our finite minds the sovereign will of God and the free will of man are separate. But in the mind of God they are one.

2. *The Analysis of Election*

Actually there are two phases to the doctrine of election. These involve, first, an elected plan; second, an elected people.

(1) *An elected plan.*—A sovereign God elected a plan of salvation. Apart from any consideration other than his redemptive and holy love, he set forth the condition by which man may receive salvation. This condition is one of grace through God's redemptive work in Christ Jesus (Rom. 11: 5; Eph. 2:8-10).

Whether or not man is saved depends upon either his acceptance or his rejection of God's elected plan. This decision takes place in the realm of man's free will. Always the initiative in redemption lies with God. But the response must be on the part of man (John 3:16-18). And man's response is either one of faith or of unbelief.

A man is condemned to death. But a sovereign state offers him a full pardon. Whether he is pardoned or not rests with his response. So it is with a sovereign God. The condition upon which he offers redemption is just and holy. The individual's response is the determining factor. The task of evangelism lies in so leading him that he will make the desired response to God's proffered gift of grace.

(2) *An elected people.*—If the redemption of one soul depends upon his response to God's elected plan, the redemption of all souls rests upon the response of God's people to his plan to elect a people for the purpose of evangelism. Furthermore, the fruitfulness of one Christian life is contingent upon his response in the same regard. These truths are seen in the progressive purpose of God in the election of his messengers.

God elected an *individual* in Noah (Gen. 6:8). He elected a *family* in Abraham (Gen. 12:1-3). The covenant with Abraham is basic in God's redemptive purpose. In it we see God's worldwide purpose of grace.

Continuing, Abraham had two sons, Ishmael and Isaac. God chose or elected Isaac (Gen. 15:4). Of Isaac's two sons God elected Jacob (Mal. 1:2-3; Rom. 9:13), and from him came the twelve tribes of Israel. In the references from Malachi and Romans love and hate relate to choice rather than to emotion. God chose the one suited for his purpose, and rejected the one who was not suited for it. Note that God's choice in each case was sovereign; the response was in man's free will.

Subsequently, God elected a *nation* (Ex. 19:1-8). Israel was to be a priest-nation to all the world. Certain conditions were laid down so that God's sovereign will bound him to the covenant only so far as Israel met those conditions. Israel's decision, then and thereafter, was in the realm of her free will. Note the "if" and "then" in Exodus 19:5.

Later, God promised a *new covenant* through Jeremiah. It was to be an inward covenant. The author of Hebrews sees this covenant as one which was sealed in the blood of Jesus Christ (Heb. 8:8-13).

Ultimately, God elected a *new people.* In Matthew 21 Jesus gave two parables designed to teach the end of the old covenant and the enactment of the new. The parable of the two sons portrays Israel as promising but not performing (Matt. 21:30). It pictures another people, at first refusing, but later agreeing to serve (Matt. 21:29). The parable of the wicked husbandman illustrates further Israel's refusal which is to be climaxed in the rejection and crucifixion of the Messiah (vv. 33-39). By the very words of the Jewish leaders (vv. 40-41) Jesus says, "The kingdom of God shall be taken from you, and given to a nation bringing forth the fruits thereof" (v. 43). "And when the chief priests and Pharisees had heard his parables, they perceived that he spake of them" (v. 45).

Therefore, it is not surprising to find that in 1 Peter 2:1-10 the apostle combines the language of Exodus 9 and Matthew 21 to write to Christian people that they are "a chosen generation; a royal priesthood, an holy nation, a peculiar people; . . . which in time past were not a people, but are now the people of God" (1 Peter 2:9-10; cf. Rom. 9-11).

Thus Christian people bear the same relationship to God under the new covenant as that borne by the nation of Israel under the old covenant. They are the new or true Israel of God, gathered out of every nation through faith in Jesus Christ.

This new covenant is one of privilege, but it involves responsibility also. That which happened to Israel may also happen to Christians, if they fail. Involved is not the loss of redemption, but of opportunity. The entire epistle to the Hebrews is a warning based upon the rebellion of Israel. Apply it to a denomination, a church, or an individual, and the lesson is the same. God never changes his sovereign purpose. But the rebellion of man's free will leads God to alter his procedure.

The Baptists of America are an illustration of this truth. In 1814 the organization of the Triennial Convention precipitated a discussion which led to a division within the body. The division was over the question of missions (evangelism).

One group held that God had elected individuals either to be saved or lost. Nothing was required of man in the matter. Thus they were antimissionary or antievangelistic. Today they have dwindled into a small, rather ineffective group. The others, on the other hand, held that God had elected a plan of salvation and a people to proclaim it. They were missionary, or evangelistic, in their outlook. Today they are the most rapidly growing of all the major denominations in America.

III. The Divine Procedure

God pursues his divine and unalterable purpose. This is the story of Christian history from Pentecost until now. It will continue to be so until the second coming of Christ.

1. *The Divine Expectation*

Hebrews 10:12-13 says: "But this man [priest], after he had offered one sacrifice for sins for ever, sat down on the right hand of God; from henceforth expecting till his enemies be made his footstool" (cf. Psalm 110:1). The Old Testament priest is never seen as seated, for his work was never done. But the priest of the new covenant is seated, symbolizing his finished work in redemption. From henceforth, until his return, he is expecting. This involves God's honoring his promise to make Jesus' enemies his footstool, his redemptive work as availing for man's salvation, and his expectation that his people will be faithful in evangelizing the world.

The day of the big football game has arrived. The coach has designed plans of attack and defense. The players have been drilled to execute them. Now they take the field. From henceforth the coach sits on the sideline, expecting. He expects every player to follow the outlined plans. He expects each man to do his best. He expects the team effort and individual performances to bring victory. He has done all that he can do. The results rest with the team.

So Jesus expects his "team" to do its best. He does not demand success but faithfulness. He knows that God will honor his promise of success, if the "team" does its best.

2. *The Divine Commission*

Standing on a mountain in Galilee Jesus gave what is known as the Great Commission (Matt. 28:19-20). He bases it upon the fact that "all power" has been given to him. Literally these words mean "out of being." Out of his very nature as the crucified and risen Lord, he gives this commission. Basically it is to "disciple" all nations (author's translation). It is a command, since Jesus used the imperative mode. Here, then, we see the sovereign God, out of the very nature of his being, giving his command. His people, on the other hand, may and must respond, either positively or negatively, in the realm of their free wills.

3. *The Divine Example*

Jesus said, "As my Father hath sent me, even so send I you" (John 20:21). God does not ask man to do what he has not done. When Jesus came it was to seek and to save that which was lost (Luke 19:10). Even though his seeking led him to Calvary, he did not turn back. In that light Hebrews says, "Wherefore . . . let us run with patience the race that is set before us, looking unto Jesus . . . who for the joy that was set before him endured the cross, despising the shame" (Heb. 12:1-2).

How Christian people shrug off this example! How little they sacrifice to tell the good news of salvation! "Ye have not yet resisted unto blood, striving against sin" (Heb. 12:4). The easily besetting sin of neglect and self-will so entangles God's people that they fall and fail in their Christian witness. The redemptive will and purpose of the eternal, almighty God waits upon his people!

FOR DISCUSSION AND CLASSWORK

1. Did God decide to redeem man after he had sinned or before? Is redemption an afterthought with God or an eternal purpose?
2. Examine the Scriptures cited under "The Eternal Aspect." Did animal sacrifice actually save men in the Old Testament, or did it point forward to a greater sacrifice?
3. Study Psalm 22 and Isaiah 53 in the light of the crucifixion. How many definite parallels are found?
4. If Jesus could not sin, were his temptations real? Compare Satan's temptations of Eve (Gen. 3) and Jesus (Matt. 4). Does Satan use any different temptations today?
5. Have several class members describe their own conversion experiences.

CHAPTER 3 OUTLINE

I. THE HOLY SPIRIT IDENTIFIED

   1. A Divine Person
   2. The Holy Spirit in the Old Testament
   3. The Holy Spirit in the New Testament
   4. The Holy Spirit as Power

II. THE HOLY SPIRIT IN THE UNSAVED

   1. The Holy Spirit Guides the Soul-Winner
   2. The Holy Spirit Enlivens the Printed Word
   3. The Holy Spirit Brings Conviction
   4. The Holy Spirit Gives Regeneration
   5. The Sin Against the Holy Spirit

III. THE HOLY SPIRIT IN THE BELIEVER

   1. The Temple of the Holy Spirit
   2. The Gifts of the Holy Spirit
   3. The Fruit of the Holy Spirit
   4. The Work of the Holy Spirit
   5. The Christian Filled with the Holy Spirit

3

The Divine Agent

THE divine agent in evangelism is the Holy Spirit. To neglect his person and work is to fail. Plans and programs are empty and futile apart from him.

Therefore, consider the divine Agent as, first, the Holy Spirit identified; second, the Holy Spirit in the unsaved; third, the Holy Spirit in the believer.

I. THE HOLY SPIRIT IDENTIFIED

In John 16:13-14 Jesus says of the Holy Spirit, "For he shall not speak of himself . . . . he shall glorify me: for he shall receive of mine, and shall shew it unto you." The Bible is quite clear in its witness concerning the Holy Spirit.

1. *A Divine Person*

The Holy Spirit is a person. The Bible refers to him as "he" (John 14:16-17, 26). He does the work of a person. He reacts as a person. Furthermore, the Holy Spirit is a divine person. Thus he is God. As Jesus was God in physical form, so the Holy Spirit is God in spiritual presence. The Scriptures ascribe to him the attributes of God: omnipresence (Psalm 139:7); omniscience (1 Cor. 2:10); and omnipotence (1 Cor. 2:11). He does the work of God (Gen. 1:2; Rom. 8:11).

Perhaps it will help to understand the Holy Spirit if he is thought of in his relationship to Jesus. Jesus said, "And I will pray the Father, and he will give you another Comforter, that he may abide with you for ever" (John 14:16). The word "another" means another of like kind. So the Holy Spirit is

31

to be another person similar to Jesus in relation to the disciples.

The difference between them is expressed in the word "that he may abide with you for ever." Jesus was with them for only a few years. The Holy Spirit will be with them forever. Jesus worked *outside* them; the Holy Spirit will work *within* them. Jesus taught them through their ears and eyes. The Holy Spirit will speak to their innermost beings.

No human pattern is sufficient to illustrate this relationship. But here is a suggestive thought. A man stands before a legal court. Which is better, to have a lawyer standing by his side to advise him, or for the man to have a legal knowledge within himself? In similar circumstances Jesus advised his disciples (John 18:11). He spoke on their behalf (John 18:8). But of the Holy Spirit he said, "But when they deliver you up, take no thought how or what ye shall speak: for it shall be given you in that same hour what ye shall speak. For it is not ye that speak, but the Spirit of your Father which speaketh in you" (Matt. 10:19-20).

2. *The Holy Spirit in the Old Testament*

The first mention of the Holy Spirit in the Old Testament is in Genesis 1:2. Thus he was active in creation. The Holy Spirit was in Joseph in Egypt (Gen. 41:38), in Bezaleel who built the tabernacle (Ex. 31:3), and in Saul, the first king of Israel (1 Sam. 10:10). Throughout the Old Testament the Holy Spirit came upon men to enable them to do mighty deeds for God. He was also related to men in the ethical and spiritual senses (Psalm 51:1; Isa. 61:1; 63:10; Ezek. 11:24).

3. *The Holy Spirit in the New Testament*

The revelation of God as Holy Spirit finds its greatest expression in the New Testament. In the Gospels the Holy Spirit is closely related to the work of Jesus: his conception (Matt. 1:18), his baptism (Matt. 3:16), his temptation

(Mark 1:12), his ministry (Luke 4:14, 16-21), his death (Heb. 9:14), and his resurrection (Rom. 1:4). Jesus sent forth his disciples in the power of the Holy Spirit (Matt. 10:16-20). He promised the Holy Spirit to them after his ascension (John 14:16-18).

The Holy Spirit came in power at Pentecost. Henceforth he worked through the Christian people in spreading the gospel throughout the earth. Acts has been called the "Gospel of the Holy Spirit."

4. The Holy Spirit as Power

The Holy Spirit is related always to God's power. He is God's power in generation (Matt. 1:18) and in regeneration (John 3:5). Jesus told his disciples to wait for the Holy Spirit's power (Luke 24:49).

When he came at Pentecost it was in a demonstration as of fire and wind. It is difficult fully to understand these figures. But worthy of note is the fact that these are basic powers in nature. Their constructive or destructive work is determined by the manner in which men relate themselves to them.

One can be completely enveloped in the Holy Spirit's power, yet realize little or no results from it. A turbine submerged in a river is powerless until the river is allowed to flow through it. The power of the Holy Spirit is abroad in the world. But until men allow this power to flow through them, the Holy Spirit is largely ineffective.

The Holy Spirit is the active agent in God's redemptive work. God the Father proposed redemption, God the Son provided it, and God the Holy Spirit propagates and activates it. However, in such activity no one person of the Godhead must be, in thought, separated from the whole of the work of redemption. The only distinction found in the Bible is with reference to the prominence of a given revelation of God at a given time.

It will be found helpful to regard God's redemptive work

as a three-act play. In Act 1 the Father is on stage, with the Son and Holy Spirit in the wings. In Act 2 the Son is on stage, with the Father and Holy Spirit in the wings. In Act 3 the Holy Spirit is on stage, with the Father and Son in the wings. But all three are one, and are present at all times.

II. THE HOLY SPIRIT IN THE UNSAVED

It is well to remember that the Holy Spirit is active in the entire spiritual experience. Evangelism involves the entire spiritual experience of man.

1. *The Holy Spirit Guides the Soul-Winner*

This truth is evident in two incidents in Acts. Acts 8:26 reads, "And the angel [messenger] of the Lord spake unto Philip, saying, Arise, and go toward the south unto the way that goeth down from Jerusalem unto Gaza." The Holy Spirit directed Philip to the place where he should meet the Ethiopian eunuch. Again in Acts 10:19-20: "While Peter thought on the vision, the Spirit said unto him, Behold three men seek thee. Arise therefore, . . . and go with them, . . . for I have sent them." Thus the Holy Spirit sent Peter to the house of Cornelius.

In both instances not only did the Holy Spirit direct the soul-winner; he also prepared the hearts of those to whom they should go. Before Philip joined himself to the chariot, the eunuch was reading the very passage from which the evangelist preached unto him Jesus (Acts 8:27-35). By the Holy Spirit Cornelius sent messengers for Peter (Acts 10: 3 ff.). So the Holy Spirit not only prepares the witness; he also makes receptive the heart of the one to whom the witness is to be given.

The author once preached in a revival in the church where he was the pastor. One afternoon, while visiting, the impression came to go to the church. Ignoring it, he continued to visit. Soon the impression almost became an audible voice.

"Go to the church!" Finally he went. Five minutes after arriving, he heard footsteps. Then a woman, whose identity he did not know, stepped through the door. "May I see the pastor?" she said.

The woman poured out her story of a life of sin. The night before she had heard the pastor preach over the radio. From that moment she had been impressed to see him. When she heard the plan of salvation, she yielded to Christ. That night she joined the church, and later was baptized. Subsequently she lived an exemplary Christian life.

Suppose that either she or he had ignored the impressions. But they did not, and she was saved. It was the work of the Holy Spirit.

2. *The Holy Spirit Enlivens the Printed Word*

As words printed on a page, the Bible would be relatively a dead thing. But by the power of the Holy Spirit it becomes alive. "For the word of God is quick [lively], and powerful, and sharper than any twoedged sword, piercing even to the dividing asunder of the soul and spirit, and the joints and marrow, and is a discerner of the thoughts and intents of the heart. Neither is there any creature that is not manifest in his sight: but all things are naked and opened unto the eyes of him with whom we have to do" (Heb. 4:12-13).

The picture is that of a physician or surgeon examining the inner parts of the human body. The chest is laid open disclosing every vital organ. In the light of modern techniques in radiology the figure is even more suggestive.

The word of God, made alive by the Holy Spirit, lays bare man's innermost being. Every organ of the soul is revealed. No microbe of sin hidden in the mind or heart can escape its searching gaze. No mere man, however eloquent or learned, can do this. Only as the Holy Spirit causes the dead page to leap into life is it made possible.

A German asked one of Billy Graham's associates to identify a piece of printed material. When told that it was a leaf from the Bible, he said: "I knew that it was something special. Nothing that I ever read affected me as this has done." It was by the work of the Holy Spirit.

3. *The Holy Spirit Brings Conviction*

It is the Holy Spirit who convicts a man of his sin. Jesus affirms this in John 16:8: "And when he [Holy Spirit] is come, he will reprove [convince, convict] the world of sin, and of righteousness, and of judgment."

(1) *"Of sin, because they believe not on me."*—The Holy Spirit enables the lost person to see sin in its true light. The sinner sees not what sin does to him only, but what it did to God. He realizes that unbelief with respect to Jesus is the greatest sin.

(2) *"Of righteousness, because I go to my Father, and ye see me no more."*—Under the power of the Holy Spirit, the lost person sees his righteousness in contrast with that of Jesus. His own righteousness appears as God sees it, as filthy rags (Isa. 64:6).

A man receives an order to appear before the king. At the appointed hour he comes, dressed in the best clothes that he has. Compared with other men he appears to be properly attired. But standing before the throne, he sees royalty robed in brilliant splendor. By comparison his own clothes are seen as they really are, filthy rags.

In infinite degree this is the experience of every person who is dressed in his own righteousness. Standing before God in the revealing light of the Holy Spirit, he sees the righteousness of God in Christ Jesus. By comparison he is ragged and dirty. Seeing how far short of God's standard of righteousness he falls, he is stripped of all self-reliance.

(3) *"Of judgment, because the prince of this world is judged."*—Here the lost person recognizes the justness of the judgment of God upon him. He is therefore ready to re-

ject Jesus, and accept hell, or else to accept Jesus, and accept heaven. Either he will rebel against God and be lost, or else he will repent of his sin and be saved.

This is the work of the Holy Spirit. Schemes and plans will not do it. Earnestness and eloquence are helpless to accomplish it.

A church can prepare for a revival, only to fail. An evangelist is secured, choirs are organized, services are advertised, pews are packed, and visitation is planned. But nothing happens. Why? Because it majored on mechanics and minored on dynamics.

4. The Holy Spirit Gives Regeneration

To Nicodemus Jesus said, "Except a man be born of water and of the Spirit, he cannot enter into the kingdom of God. Ye must be born again" (John 3:5, 7).

Various interpreters find different meanings in the words "born of the water." Most certainly they do not refer to Christian baptism. The author sees them as referring to the natural birth (cf. John 3:4, 6). Nicodemus confused the natural with the spiritual birth. Jesus tells him that one must be born naturally before he can be born spiritually. Natural birth alone is not enough. "Ye must be born again" (John 3:7).

The words of importance here are "born. . . of the Spirit." A physician may say, "If you will explain the spiritual birth so that I can understand it, I will become a Christian." In reply one can say to him, "If you will explain the natural birth, then I will explain the spiritual birth."

This is exactly the point that Jesus made. Neither can be explained by finite minds. Men can only co-operate in both. But in each the result is seen (cf. John 3:8).

Jesus answered that the spiritual birth is the work of the Holy Spirit. From conviction and repentance he leads the lost person, through faith in Jesus, to an experience of regeneration. Furthermore, he seals the believer unto redemption (2 Cor. 1:21-22; Eph. 1:13-14). He also gives to him the assurance of salvation (1 John 4:4-12).

5. *The Sin Against the Holy Spirit*

At this point it is well to consider briefly the sin against the Holy Spirit (Matt. 12:27-37). Jesus was performing miracles by the power of the Holy Spirit. The Pharisees attributed this power to Satan. Jesus said that this blasphemy against the Holy Spirit constituted an unpardonable sin.

It would seem that it is possible for one to become so crystallized in sin that it is impossible for him to recognize the work of God for his salvation. This sin need not necessarily be of an immoral nature. As with the Pharisees, it may more readily be one of intellect or pride. It most certainly is in the realm of persistent unbelief with regard to Jesus. Why is this sin unpardonable? Does God's anger become such that he refuses to pardon? To say this would hardly be in keeping with the revealed nature of God.

Dr. B. H. Carroll explained it in this manner: If one blasphemes or hardens his heart toward God the Father, he still has Jesus and the Holy Spirit. If he blasphemes Jesus, he has the Holy Spirit. If he hardens his heart against the Holy Spirit, there is no one left. The Holy Spirit convicts of sin. But God says that his Spirit will not strive with man always (Gen. 6:3).

The sin against the Holy Spirit is one of the greatest obstacles encountered by the soul-winner. Thinking that he has committed this sin, a person does not try to believe in Jesus. But such a feeling is proof that he has not so sinned. For his consciousness of sin proves that the Holy Spirit is still striving with him.

The lost person who says that he has no sin for which he needs forgiveness is a more likely candidate. Certainly unbelief, caused by moral or spiritual hardness, and persisted in until death, is unpardonable in this world or the world to come. No Christian can commit this sin.

III. THE HOLY SPIRIT IN THE BELIEVER

Regeneration does not mark the end of evangelism. It has been noted that the birth of a child only serves to add a greater responsibility to his parents. So it is in regeneration.

The Holy Spirit is vital in this continuing experience. As a parent watches over and provides for the child, as the teacher guides and inspires the pupil, so does the Holy Spirit do for the Christian.

1. *The Temple of the Holy Spirit*

The Holy Spirit indwells the believer. This Jesus declared when he said, "For he dwelleth with you, and shall be in you" (John 14:17). The word "dwelleth" means to abide or to sojourn in one. So when a person becomes a Christian, the Holy Spirit comes to stay in that person's life.

This truth is further stated in 1 Corinthians 3:16: "Know ye not that . . . the Spirit of God dwelleth in you?" (cf. 1 Cor. 3:17; 6:19; 2 Cor. 6:16). Here the word "dwelleth" is a word meaning to make one's home with one. So the Holy Spirit is at home in the Christian.

A Christian is heard praying for the Holy Spirit to indwell him. Such a prayer is unnecessary. The Holy Spirit is already there. He only waits to be used. A church sings, "Let the Holy Spirit come and take control." The word "come" is unnecessary. He has come already. He only wishes to be permitted to "take control." However, if the person is not a Christian, the song is correct.

2. *The Gifts of the Holy Spirit*

In 1 Corinthians 12 to 14 Paul deals with this matter. After setting forth the differences in spiritual gifts, he proceeds to list them: "wisdom," or intelligence practically used;

"knowledge," insight or illumination; "faith," wonder-working faith; "healing," acts of healing; "miracles," working of powers such as healing; "prophecy," a speaking forth of God's message; "discerning" of spirits, ability to distinguish between divine or diabolical spirits; "tongues," languages; "interpretation of tongues," ability to interpret a foreign language to those present (1 Cor. 12:8-10).[1]

Strangely enough, these gifts became the source of divisions within the Corinthian church. Apparently each person insisted that his gift was the most important. This, of course, was an abuse of the gifts of the Holy Spirit.

The use, or abuse, of some of these gifts was censured by Paul. Ecstatic gifts such as miracles, healing, and tongues were the most noteworthy ones. But even faith, wisdom, knowledge, and prophecy were regarded by Paul as falling in the same category if they became the cause of undue pride (1 Cor. 13:1-3). To the apostle "love" was the greatest gift. Apart from it all gifts are meaningless.

Some of these gifts, especially miracles, healings, and tongues, were temporary in nature. They belonged to the early stage of Christianity (1 Cor. 13:11). These were given as signs (cf. John 2:11) that God was in the Christian movement. "Tongues," in particular, was treated in such a category. The word "unknown" is not in the original text. "Tongues" means languages. It was simply the ability to speak in a foreign language without having studied it. It was a temporary gift of the Holy Spirit to effect the rapid spread of Christianity (Acts 2:6-11).

The author visited language schools on several mission fields. The missionaries were laboriously learning to speak the languages of the people with whom they would work. But in the first century there was neither time nor opportunity for language schools. If one asks why modern missionaries

1. A. T. Robertson, *Word Pictures in the New Testament,* IV (Nashville: Baptist Sunday School Board, 1931), 169-170.

are not given the gift of "tongues," the answer is that the Holy Spirit works as he chooses to work (John 3:8). He does not so choose to work today.

Even in the first century Paul discounted the abiding value of such gifts. Like a flower which buds, blossoms, and then falls away, so, said Paul, shall it be with these ecstatic gifts (1 Cor. 13:8-10). They will make their intended contribution and then pass away. Apart from faith, hope, and love, Paul commends only one gift, prophecy (1 Cor. 14:1). While he urges the permission of speaking in tongues, in that day, he says to covet to prophesy (1 Cor. 14:39). "Prophecy" is not so much the ability to foretell as it is to tell forth the gospel. The Holy Spirit still endows individuals with gifts, or abilities, which enable them to become useful parts of the body of Christ (1 Cor. 12:11-31).

Each reader would do well to study carefully 1 Corinthians 12 to 14, that he may comprehend Paul's teaching more fully. More important, he should through prayer and self-analysis discover and devote to God the gifts which the Holy Spirit has deposited in him.

3. *The Fruit of the Holy Spirit*

In Galatians 5:22-25 Paul lists the fruit of the Holy Spirit which would be evident in the lives of those who lived and walked in the Spirit. "Love" is the governing principle of life. "Joy" is an inner condition independent of outward environment. "Peace" is an inner calm in the face of adversity. "Longsuffering" is the patience to suffer wrong without seeking revenge. "Gentleness" is kindness actively engaged in helping others, even those who would do harm. "Goodness" is both purity of life and unselfish service. "Faith" is loyalty to men and God. "Meekness" is strength in the inner self. "Temperance" is self-control.

These are the true gifts of the Holy Spirit which should be earnestly coveted (1 Cor. 12:31). They are not glamorous but they make effective the Christian life in its witness for Christ.

One meets a Christian for the first time. There is nothing beautiful about his appearance or captivating about his personality. But he is said to bear acquaintance. The truth is that as one comes to know him, certain qualities of life appear which transform him into a winsome personality.

4. *The Work of the Holy Spirit*

The Holy Spirit is actively at work with and through those who are yielded to him. For practical purposes this work may be regarded as threefold.

(1) *Comforter.*—In John 14:16 Jesus calls the Holy Spirit "Comforter." This is the word 'paraclete." It means one called alongside. Sometimes it referred to a lawyer, especially for the defense.

The Holy Spirit comforts in sorrow, encourages in disappointment, and emboldens in the face of adversity. He gives the "peace of God, which passeth all understanding" (Phil. 4:7; cf. John 14:26-27). Paul, in prison, could share the peace that was in his heart. This is by the work of the Holy Spirit.

(2) *Counselor.*—The Holy Spirit "shall teach you all things, and bring all things to your remembrance, whatsoever I have said unto you" (John 14:26). Here is the explanation both of the four Gospels and of the other New Testament writings. This is further affirmed in John 16:13.

This truth is significant for those who aspire to witness for Christ. The Holy Spirit guides the preacher or teacher in his study of God's Word. He makes the brain fertile and the tongue eloquent. He speaks through the soul-winner as he deals with one lost soul.

The churches of a city were engaged in a visitation-evangelism campaign. The director said: "When you ring the first door bell, you will be frightened to death. I hope so, for then you will be able to do your best work." As the visitors returned to make their reports, there was a gleam of triumphant joy in their eyes. One by one they reported their feelings as the director had said they would. But once they began, with fumbling words, to speak to their prospects, words seemed to flow from a heart of eagerness, words touched as by a divine fire. No wonder that many souls were won that week. One church reported ninety-five additions on the following Sunday. It was the work of the Counselor, the Holy Spirit.

(3) *Administrator.*—The Holy Spirit works not only with and through the individual, but he also directs the broader activities of evangelistic endeavor.

In every new development in the spread of first-century Christianity, the Holy Spirit was the moving force. In this light study the following references: Acts 8:26, 39; 10:2, 44-47; 11:21, 24; 13:2, 52; 16:6-10; 18:9; 23:11; 27:23-24. He directed the preaching of the gospel to Samaritans, half-Jews; to the Ethiopian eunuch, a proselyte; and to Cornelius, a God-fearer or Gentile who studied the Jewish religion but was not an adherent of it. He led in the preaching of the gospel to the Greeks, in sending the first missionaries, and guided them throughout their ever-widening ministry. From that day until the present, the Holy Spirit has continued to guide the individual soul-winner, even as he directs the affairs of the greatest mission board.

The author once served on a committee to nominate an executive secretary for the Southern Baptist Foreign Mission Board. After much deliberation, the suggestion was made that after prayer each member write on a piece of paper the name which he was impressed to suggest. It was found that each member had written the name of M. Theron Rankin. It was a holy moment, for each member felt that the Holy Spirit had led in his choice.

5. *The Christian Filled with the Holy Spirit*

In Ephesians 5:18 Paul says, "And be not drunk with wine, wherein is excess; but be filled with the Spirit." This latter is also Jesus' command (Luke 24:49). Men sometimes look to alcoholic beverages to give them a temporary "lift." Paul says that the Christian is to live an exhilarated life by being filled with the Spirit. This is a timely and timeless word.

A man who is "drunk with wine" does not need to advertise the fact. It will show in his bodily appearance and conduct. The Spirit-filled Christian need not forever be speaking of it. That also will be revealed in his life. Indeed, the person who makes a boast of being filled with the Holy Spirit may contrariwise be filled with inordinate pride. Jesus never boasted of the Spirit's presence in his life. Yet no one will deny such a presence. It showed in his every attitude, word, and deed.

The greatest constructive forces in life are those silent powers which work without ostentation. Gentle breezes do not roar yet they bear pollen from one plant to another, making possible abundant harvests. Mighty rivers flow gently as they bear the commerce of nations. Tides silently lift ocean liners where groaning machines fail. The brain of Albert Einstein made no noise in its amazing computations, but it lifted man's horizon beyond his fondest dreams.

So the Christian who is filled with the Holy Spirit lets his light "so shine before men, that they may see [his] good works, and glorify [his] Father which is in heaven" (Matt. 5:16). This kind of person is God's most effective human instrument in the work of evangelism.

FOR DISCUSSION AND CLASSWORK

1. How are the three persons related in the Trinity? Is the Holy Spirit as important as the other two persons?

2. Is it better to have the Holy Spirit today than to have walked with Jesus when he was on earth?

3. Ask the class members to relate incidents when the Holy Spirit guided them in soul-winning.

4. Discuss the sin against the Holy Spirit in the light of Matthew 12 : 27-37.

5. Examine the passage relating to the use of "tongues" in the New Testament. Why is the word "unknown" italicized in 1 Corinthians 14 : 2, 4, 13, 14, 19, 27?

CHAPTER 4 OUTLINE

I. THE INVOLVED PERSONALITIES
   1. The Gift of God
   2. The Act of Man
   3. The Work of God and Man

II. THE INVOLVED OBLIGATION
   1. The Obligation of Growth
   2. The Obligation Neglected
   3. The Will Challenged

III. THE INVOLVED CONSEQUENCES
   1. The Name of God Blasphemed
   2. The Opportunity of Man Lost
   3. The Redemptive Purpose of God Delayed

4

The Human Response

GOD never does by a miracle what he can do through a man. Thus even God is dependent upon his people. This truth is fundamental so far as evangelism is concerned.

If salvation involved only the sovereign will of God, the entire matter would have been concluded in the Garden of Eden. But because the free will of man is involved, the matter is more complicated. The work of God must wait upon the will of man.

It is well, therefore, to consider the human response in evangelism. This includes, first, the involved personalities; second, the involved obligation; third, the involved consequences.

I. THE INVOLVED PERSONALITIES

The personalities involved in evangelism are God and man. If there is a Godward side, there is also a manward side. Simply stated, on the Godward side there is a gift; on the manward side there is the reception or rejection of the gift.

1. *The Gift of God*

The basis of evangelism is a gift from God. In Romans 6 : 23 Paul says, "For the wages of sin is death; but the gift of God is eternal life through Jesus Christ our Lord." "Gift" is the key word here. As opposed to "wages," something earned, eternal life is a gift. "Wages" is the word for a soldier's pay. But "gift" is also a military word. On special occasions a Roman emperor gave his soldiers a free grant of money, a free gift. They received it, not for services rendered, but out of the goodness of the emperor's heart. He did so only for his friends. However, God's gift is offered to his enemies. This is affirmed in Romans 5:8, "But God commendeth his love toward us, in that, while we were yet sinners, Christ died for us."

This word "gift" is one of the big words in Paul's theology. It is used fourteen times by him.

A kindred word to this one is the word "grace." It also is a favorite word of Paul. Of one hundred and fifty-six times in the New Testament, Paul uses it one hundred and two times. Its principal meaning is in reference to God's merciful kindness exerted upon souls in turning to Christ, and to the development of their faith, knowledge, and love in Christ. Grace, therefore, is involved in every phase of evangelism.

(1) *Salvation by grace*.—The initial experience of regeneration is a gift from God. In Romans 3:23-24 Paul affirms this: "For all have sinned, and come short of the glory of God; being justified freely by his grace through the redemption that is in Christ Jesus."

This truth is even more emphatically asserted in Ephesians 2:8-9: "For by grace are ye saved through faith; and that not of yourselves: it is the gift of God: not of works, lest any man should boast" (cf. Rom. 5:15, 20-21). The word "gift" in this verse translates another word meaning present. So by the grace of God man receives regeneration as a present.

A man in the employ of another performs a duty assigned to him. He then can demand payment for his services, even by law if necessary. But if this same employer, out of the goodness of his heart, presents him a gift, his only reaction can be one of gratitude. It is on this latter basis alone that man can receive regeneration. God is under no obligation to redeem him. It is a matter of grace from beginning to end (cf. John 1:16). Man's only reasonable response is one of gratitude and faith.

(2) *The gifts of grace.*—This refers to those qualities and abilities which God bestows upon the Christian, through the Holy Spirit, to fit him for God's service. Paul speaks of these in 1 Corinthians 12:4: "Now there are diversities of gifts, but the same Spirit." "Gifts" in this passage is the same word mentioned above as being akin to the word for grace.

In the Corinthian church these gifts became the cause of individual pride, resulting in confusion. Paul reminds them of the unreasonableness of their attitude. "For who maketh thee to differ [distinguisheth thee] from another? and what hast thou that thou didst not receive? now if thou didst receive it, why dost thou glory, as if thou hadst not received it?" (1 Cor. 4:7).

If one person can sing, teach, or preach better than others, he has no cause to be proud. Instead, that ability should humble him in the realization that God has entrusted him with such a gift. In 1 Corinthians 12:14-24 Paul states that each is important in the fulfilment of the ministry of the churches.

One of the most useful men in a certain church was a lowly person as society rates men. His one talent was a big smile and a hearty handshake. But he used it for God's glory. At every stated service he was at the church door, shaking hands and making people welcome. No one could go away saying that in that church he was not greeted properly.

2. *The Act of Man*

The gifts of God are dependent upon the response of man. Man may either receive them or reject them. His response makes the gift either effective or ineffective. This is true whether the gift be regeneration or sanctification.

(1) *Faith.*—This response refers primarily to man's acceptance of God's redeeming work. Paul so states in Ephesians 2:8. "Grace" is God's act in giving. "Faith" is man's response in receiving the gift.

The apostle enlarges upon this thought in Romans 4. Even Abraham was saved by faith apart from works. "Abraham believed God, and it was counted unto him for righteousness" (Rom. 4:3; cf. Rom. 10:2-4). The word "counted" is a bookkeeping term. Abraham's faith was put down in the ledger of God as righteousness or justification (cf. John 3:16-18; Acts 16:31).

In the first century, as now, there were those who insisted that salvation was by faith plus works (cf. Acts 15). Naturally this teaching negated the gospel of grace. Hence the repeated emphasis of the New Testament writers upon faith as the means of appropriating salvation (cf. Romans and Galatians).

Faith implies intellectual belief with regard to the gospel story. But it involves also the action of the will, as expressed in trust, acceptance, and committal.

(2) *Dedication.*—Here the response is related to the spiritual gifts which are bestowed upon the Christian. Earlier it was noted that the Holy Spirit endows each Christian with certain abilities. The lack of a proper dedication of the gifts of God may result in confusion and schism within the church.

It is at this point that some people are confused over the teachings of the New Testament regarding faith and works. Over against salvation by grace through faith are the words of James: "What doth it profit, my brethren, though a man say he hath faith, and have not works? can faith save him? . . . faith without works is dead" (James 2:14, 20). Two things may be said about this. First, James is saying that a saving faith will express itself in works (cf. Eph. 2:10). Second, the word "saved" involves sanctification as well as justification. A justification which is through faith expresses itself through subsequent works (cf. Luke 3:8-14; James 2:21-26). This truth Paul affirms when he urges the Roman Christians to present their bodies to God as instruments of righteousness (Rom. 6:12-18; 12:1).

Dedication is further seen in the parable of the talents (Matt. 25:14-30). By grace the owner entrusted certain talents to three servants according to their several abilities. In faith each received the gift. Two dedicated themselves to a rightful use of the talents. One failed to do so. The faithful ones needed only sixteen words to report their faithfulness. The unfaithful steward needed forty-three words to explain his failure. God is not interested in excuses but in results!

This parable is both timely and timeless. A singer dissipates his talent for selfish ends. A teacher refuses to teach without a large class. A man fails to recognize his wealth as a trust from God. A salesman sells his wares but neglects to tell lost people about the Saviour. Conversely, others dedicate their talents to God, and men are blessed thereby. The gifts are the same but the response is different.

3. *The Work of God and Man*

The gifts of God involve both God and man. In regeneration God offers but man must receive. In sanctification God bestows but man must develop and use. Even in this latter instance God works in man to bring about the desired result. "For by the grace of God I am what I am: and his grace which was bestowed upon me was not in vain; but I laboured more abundantly than they all; yet not I, but the grace of God which was with me" (1 Cor. 15:10). In this light Paul wrote to the Philippian Christians: "Work out your own salvation with fear and trembling. For it is God which worketh in you both to will and to do of his good pleasure" (2:12-13). It is man working out what God has already worked in him.

II. THE INVOLVED OBLIGATION

It is evident that the present obligation rests upon the Christian. God has made an investment in each one. What each person does with it rests within himself. Regeneration is a gift. But sanctification is both a gift from God and an accomplishment on the part of man. Therefore, the Christian is under obligation both to God and men (cf. Rom. 1:1, 14-15).

1. *The Obligation of Growth*

The Christian is obligated to grow into the Christian character which God intends that he shall be. The last words written for us by Peter confirm this: "But grow in grace, and in the knowledge of our Lord and Saviour Jesus Christ. To him be glory both now and for ever. Amen" (2 Peter 3:18). The word "grow" means to keep on growing. There is never a point in this life when the Christian is to cease doing so.

This truth is affirmed by Jesus. When he said, "Ye must be born again" (John 3:7), he drew a picture of an infant, needing food, exercise, and instruction, in order to grow into a fully grown man (cf. Eph. 4:11-15). In Matthew 11:28-29 he reiterated this truth: "Come unto me, all ye that labour and are heavy laden, and I will give you rest." Here is regeneration. But there is more. "Take my yoke upon you, and learn of me. . . ." In Jesus' day to take a yoke referred to a pupil coming under the instruction of a teacher. In the Christian sense regeneration is enrolment or taking the yoke. Henceforth, the process of learning and development is involved.

Thus is seen the obligation for growth which is placed upon the Christian. Generally speaking, a person grows physically by eating, breathing, and exercise. A Christian is to feed upon the Word of God. He is to develop his powers through spiritual endeavor. In the same sense he grows intellectually. He must receive instruction from God's Word. He must comprehend it through the Holy Spirit. He must express it in the practical outworkings of his Christian life.

A little baby is beautiful but if twenty-one years later he is still an infant, physically and intellectually, that is quite another matter. An eager-eyed child, on the day of enrolment, is a delight to the teacher. But if years later he is a dullard in the first grade, he is a disappointment beyond measure.

This truth also places an obligation upon the churches. The task of evangelism is not completed when a person is won to Christ. It has only begun in the larger sense of the word salvation. The soul has been redeemed. But the life must be saved also. Herein is the greatest failure in the work of the churches.

A little girl said, "Mother, I wish that I had never joined the church." Alarmed, the mother asked why. "Because," answered her daughter, "before I joined the church, everyone was interested in me. Now no one ever pays any attention to me." Alas, how often this is true!

2. The Obligation Neglected

This obligation is neglected both by the individual Christian and by the churches. A man was heard to say, "If I can just be saved, and be assured a place in heaven, that is enough for me." A pastor remarked, "It is my job to preach the gospel, not to run the Sunday school." Out of mistaken zeal, both had missed the larger sense of salvation. Such an attitude results in at least two tragic conditions.

(1) *Doctrinal instability.*—In Galatians 1:6 Paul says, "I marvel that ye are so soon removed from him that called you into the grace of Christ unto another gospel." The word "another" means another of different kind. Paul preached a gospel of salvation by grace through faith. These people had fallen victim to those who preached another kind of gospel, by faith plus works.

This is also a present-day problem. The adherents of "another kind of gospel" make greater inroads than some would imagine. A man died without becoming a Christian. His wife, a Baptist, lamented, "I am so sorry that he was never baptized!" Too often one hears of some Sunday school pupil becoming enraged because the teacher dared to contradict the teaching of another denomination. One person was heard to remark: "I do not think we should disturb heathen people. They have their religion, just as we have ours." The ecumenical movement has made greater progress within the thinking of many Christian people than outer, organic separation would indicate.

A pastor emphasized this fact. He told of being in widely separated cities where he found former leaders in his church to be active members of churches of other denominations. This is due to what Paul said in Ephesians 4:14. They have been "tossed to and fro, and carried about with every wind of doctrine, by the sleight of men, and cunning craftiness whereby they lie in wait to deceive." This is because churches have not edified the body of Christ. Multitudes of Christians have not "come in [into] the unity of the faith, and of the [full] knowledge of the Son of God, unto a perfect [complete, adult] man, unto the measure of the stature of the fulness of Christ" (Eph. 4:13).

(2) *Ineffective Christians.*—The author of Hebrews affirms this. "For when for the time ye ought to be teachers, ye have need that one teach you again which be the first principles [ABC's] of the oracles of God; and are become such as have need of milk, and not of strong meat. For every one that useth milk is unskilful [has no experience] in the word of righteousness: for he is [keeps on being] a babe. But strong meat belongeth to them that are of full age [adults], even those who by reason of use have their senses exercised [as in a gymnasium] to discern both good and evil" (Heb. 5:12-14).

This last thought suggests Christian lives made ineffective by sinful living. The greater burden of the passage rests upon those who are good, but good-for-nothing. As babes they require constant attention. Failing to receive it, they set up a howl. Even those who would be active in soul-winning, pastor and teacher alike, must spend precious time coddling these babes in Christ.

These babes are a liability in the work of the Lord. They eat, but never feed. They demand, and give not. They must be ministered unto, but never minister. In grading, the "nursery" should end after age three. But, alas, it extends from the cradle to the grave!

3. *The Will Challenged*

This the author of Hebrews does when he says, "Therefore leaving the principles [ABC's] of the doctrine of Christ, *let us go on* unto perfection" (Heb. 6:1 author's italics). This italicized phrase is the theme of Hebrews. Instead of being a warning to first-century Christians against going back into Judaism, it is a challenge for them to go on unto the fulfilment of God's will for their lives in world missions, or evangelism.[1]

God grant that every Christian, every church, will read and act upon Hebrews 6:3: "And this will we do, if God permit."

III. THE INVOLVED CONSEQUENCES

At least three consequences of failure are mentioned.

1. *The Name of God Blasphemed*

What Paul said of the Jew applies equally to the Christian (Rom. 2:17-24). Making his boast of God, knowing God's will, presuming to be a teacher of babes and a guide to the blind, yet he lives either in positively open sin or in negative idleness. What is the result? "For the name of God is blasphemed among the Gentiles [lost people] through you" (Rom. 2:24).

1. See Herschel H. Hobbs, *Studies in Hebrews* (Nashville: Convention Press, 1954).

Why is the influence of the Christian cause so weak, the voice of the pulpit so ineffective? Why do the forces of corruption and evil in society laugh at the preacher who condemns evil? It is because the trumpet of Christian lives gives an uncertain sound. The principles of God's righteousness and justice have not been allowed to come into close grips with the problems of daily living. Too often one's religion is a cloak to be worn to church, but is never worn where cross the crowded ways of life.

2. *The Opportunity of Man Lost*

What is even more serious, Christianity, collectively and individually, loses its opportunity. God's redemptive purpose will succeed. A given generation of Christians may delay it. But it will not defeat it. The tragedy is that that generation loses its opportunity to be used of God.

The same thing is true of the individual. In the parable of the talents, those who were faithful were rewarded (Matt. 25:21, 23). But of the servant who failed, Jesus said, "Take therefore the talent from him, . . . from him that hath not shall be taken away even that which he hath" (Matt. 25:28-29). The owner did not lose his property, but the servant lost his opportunity. This truth Jesus affirmed elsewhere. "For whosoever will save his life shall lose it" (Luke 9:24). This is true, whether one thinks of the soul or of the usefulness of the Christian life.

Five times the author of Hebrews exhorts against failure to live up to one's opportunity in God's redemptive purpose (cf. 2:1-3; 3:7 ff.; 6:1 ff.; 10:19 ff.; 12:1 ff.). It will suffice to examine only one. In Hebrews 2:1 the author says, "Therefore we ought to give the more earnest heed to the things which we have heard, lest at any time we should let them slip." This is an unfortunate translation. "Let them slip" renders a word meaning to flow by. In its particular form here it means "lest we be flowed by." The picture is of one who is stationary. As the river flows on, the person on its banks is flowed by.

This is true of denominations, churches, and individual Christians. The river of God's redemptive purpose flows on. But those who refuse to be carried along by it are flowed by, or left behind. This refers not to regeneration but to Christian opportunity, for those to whom the author of Hebrews is writing are already born again.

3. The Redemptive Purpose of God Delayed

The consequences of the Christian's refusal to shoulder his obligation are broader than his own opportunity. They involve the progress of God's redemptive purpose. When Israel refused to enter the land of Canaan, she did not thwart God's purpose. But she delayed it for a generation.

The same is true today. The cause of Christ goes forward on leadened feet. The Dark Ages of Europe were characterized by a dearth of Christian witness. This so-called enlightened age fights what sometimes seems to be a losing battle against the encroachments of Satan. While multitudes of Christians dawdle, other multitudes die without Christ as their Saviour.

The present generation of Christians is the connecting link between all that God has done and all that he wills to do in the future. This is the meaning of Hebrews 11:39-40: "And these all [past heroes of faith], having obtained a good report through faith, received not the promise: God having provided [foreseen] some better thing for us, that they without us should not be made perfect [complete]." What they did will not avail, except in their own generations. The unbroken witness depends upon this present generation.

A wrecker goes down the street pulling an automobile. Connecting the two is a tow chain. By it the power of one motor is transferred to the other car. But suppose one link is missing from the chain. The wrecker goes on, but the car is left behind. The illustration leaves much to be desired. But at the point of the missing link, it is suggestive indeed.

It has taken almost two thousand years for the Christian witness to achieve what it has. How long would it take for the world to lapse into stark paganism? Less than a hundred years! All that is necessary is for the Christian witness to cease for that long.

Some years ago an enthusiastic group marched under the banner "Win the world to Christ in this generation." The world must be won to Christ in every generation!

No generation may regard itself as an end unto itself unless it would become the last generation. Within each generation is the power to reproduce itself. It is not merely its privilege but its responsibility to do so. That which is true in generation is equally the case in regeneration.

In a very real sense the process of evangelism begins anew with every new baby that is born. The very act of birth is God's way of saying to the parents, "Take this child and rear him for me." No wise parent will simply assume that the child will be fed, clothed, and educated. Instead he sees his responsibility to make positive efforts to this end. This must also be true in spiritual matters. And just as the former responsibility must be assumed not by the parents alone but by the community also, so must the latter responsibility include the larger circle of spiritual institutions. This is particularly true with regard to the churches. Only as the home and the church co-operate in this spiritual enterprise may the cause of Christ go forward unbroken and unabated.

FOR DISCUSSION AND CLASSWORK

1. What is meant by the sovereignty of God? How is it related to man's free will?

2. If redemption is a gift, what is the relation between works and grace?
3. Is regeneration the ultimate goal of the Christian experience?
4. Suggest ways in which the Christian may dishonor God.
5. Why is God's redemptive purpose dependent upon man?

CHAPTER 5 OUTLINE

I. THE PRINCIPLES INVOLVED
1. The Moral Attributes of God
2. The Plight of Man
3. The Saving Ministry of Jesus

II. THE PATTERN FOLLOWED
1. The Threefold Ministry of Jesus
2. Jesus Seeking the Lost
3. Jesus Developing the Saved

III. THE GOAL ENVISIONED
1. The Intermediate Conquest
2. The Great Commission
3. The Condition and Result

5

The New Testament Principles and Pattern

[*In the Ministry of Jesus*]

NEW TESTAMENT churches recognize Jesus as Lord. Therefore, any program of evangelism which they follow must take into account the pattern which he designed. This pattern is not mechanical but spiritual. It involves definite principles and procedures, but the framework itself is never in the forefront. It may best be described in the words from Isaiah 61:1-2, which Jesus appropriated unto himself at the beginning of his public ministry.

"The Spirit of the Lord is upon me, because he hath anointed me to preach the gospel to the poor; he hath sent me to heal the brokenhearted, to preach deliverance to the captives, and recovering of sight to the blind, to set at liberty them that are bruised, to preach the acceptable year of the Lord" (Luke 4:18-19). In this light, note, first, the principles involved; second, the pattern followed; third, the goal envisioned.

I. THE PRINCIPLES INVOLVED

Jesus' pattern of evangelism involves certain abiding principles which he knew to be inherent in the nature both of God and of man. They are related to his ministry as cause is to effect. For a proper understanding of New Testament evangelism these principles must be considered.

1. *The Moral Attributes of God*

Attributes are those qualities which describe the character of God. Theologians usually list them as four in number.

(1) *Holiness.*—Jesus assumed God as holy. Only one time did he speak of him as such. In John 17:11 he addressed God as "Holy Father." This suggests not only the moral character of God, but his exalted nature as well (Isa. 6:1-3). Furthermore, this attribute speaks of God's dedication of himself to his redemptive purpose as it relates to man.

(2) *Righteousness.*—Only one time did Jesus address his Father as "righteous" (John 17:25). But everywhere this attribute is assumed. It speaks of God's self-affirmation on behalf of the right as opposed to the wrong. In the Bible God's righteousness is presented as mandatory, as seen in the Ten Commandments; punitive, God's administering of justice; and redemptive. All of these are associated both with Jesus' reference to the character of God, and with his own redemptive ministry.

(3) *Truth.*—In John 17:17 Jesus prays that his disciples may be sanctified in "thy truth: thy word is truth." This speaks of God as the source and basis of all forms of knowing, and of all objects of knowledge. Thus God's will is the very essence and criteria of truth. It suggests that which God requires of man in every facet of his being.

(4) *Love.*—This refers to the self-giving of God, whereby he seeks the highest good for the object of his love. It expresses his divine nature, which calls for a like response from other free, moral, and intelligent beings. "For God so loved the world, that he gave his only begotten Son, that whosoever believeth in him should not perish, but have everlasting life." (John 3:16; cf. John 17:24, 26). Like God's holiness, love permeates all of the other attributes of God, and colors his every activity.

In all of Jesus' references to God there is not one note of

undue familiarity. Though he was the Son of God, even God himself, he never regarded deity other than in an attitude of supreme reverence. To him God was not "the Man upstairs." Or as one movie actress said, "When you get to know him, he is a living Doll." Such attitudes ignore the nature and character of God altogether.

2. The Plight of Man

Over against the character of God Jesus placed man. And his analysis of man is true (John 2:25).

(1) *The depraved nature.*—Jesus knew man to be totally depraved in his nature. This he affirmed in John 8:44: "Ye are of your father the devil, and the lusts of your father ye will do." Thus man does not possess a marred image which needs to be improved. He has a corrupt nature which must be changed (Matt. 23:25-28). Regardless of a man's position or personal attainments, of him Jesus said, "Except a man be born again, he cannot see the kingdom of God" (John 3:3). Our Lord never taught reformation, but regeneration.

Jesus regarded him as of infinite worth (Mark 8:36). Though man is lost from God (Luke 15), his salvation is so worthy an enterprise as to call for God's mightiest work to seek and to save him (Luke 19:10).

This attitude should possess every child of God. The Bible does not say that some have sinned, and come short of the glory of God, but that all have done so. Outside of Christ the Junior child is lost. The cultured lady is lost. The wealthy banker is lost. The scholar is lost. A person can go to hell behind a mahogany desk as quickly as behind a lathe, from the cloistered halls of a university as from the raucous atmosphere of a brothel. Rescue missions are found on Skid Row. Evangelism must center its mission of rescue in the community of palatial mansions as well.

(2) *The insufficiency of the law.*—That Jesus regarded the

keeping of the Mosaic law as insufficient in changing the depraved nature of man is affirmed in Matthew 5:20: "For I say unto you, That except your righteousness shall exceed the righteousness of the scribes and Pharisees, ye shall in no case enter into the kingdom of heaven." The scribes and Pharisees were meticulous in their efforts to keep the law of Moses (Matt. 23:23). According to Jesus, publicans and harlots who believed in him would precede the scribes and Pharisees into the kingdom of God (Matt. 21:31-32).

Jesus pointed out that even Bible study alone cannot suffice for salvation. To the Jews he said: "[Ye] search the scriptures; for in them ye think ye have eternal life: and they are they which testify of me. And ye will not come to me, that ye might have life" (John 5:39-40).

The same may be said of any other rote exercise in religion. Too many Sunday school teachers regard the enrolment of pupils and the teaching of a lesson as the fulfilment of their responsibility. These are but means to an end. Except they bear fruit in regeneration, and in Christian growth, they are meaningless exercises.

Thus Jesus emphasized the need for man's regeneration. Someone said that the well cannot be purified simply by painting the pump. It is said that when a woman is depressed, she should buy herself a new hat. Facetious? Yet many adopt this principle in spiritual matters. An evil nature cannot be changed simply by donning a new hat or a new suit of clothes. Jesus affirmed this when he said: "Woe unto you, scribes and Pharisees, hypocrites! for ye are like unto whited sepulchres, which indeed appear beautiful outward, but are within full of dead men's bones, and of all uncleanness. Even so ye also outwardly appear righteous unto men, but within ye are full of hypocrisy and iniquity" (Matt. 23:27-28).

This is an apt description. It was the Passover season. The tombs about Jerusalem were painted white, lest anyone should touch them, and thus, through defilement, become unfit to observe the feast.

(3) *The only hope.*—To Jesus man's only hope lay in a vital faith in Christ. This he declared in John 3:18: "He that believeth on him is not condemned: but he that believeth not is condemned already, because he hath not believed in the name of the only begotten Son of God." This was said not to a moral leper, but to a paragon of virtue.

As Peter Cartwright, the Methodist evangelist, once preached of man's condemnation in sin, General Andrew Jackson entered the church. Someone in the congregation whispered a little loudly, "General Jackson has come in." Fixing his eyes on General Jackson, the preacher declared, "Who is General Jackson? If he don't get his soul converted, God will damn him as quick as he would a Guinea Negro."

3. *The Saving Ministry of Jesus*

In his incarnation Jesus revealed God in his true nature (Matt. 20:28; John 14:9). He fulfilled the true meaning of the Law (Matt. 5:17). In his death he satisfied the demands of the Law. And in his resurrection God gave him victory over death (Luke 24:5-8). Thus he is able to save to the uttermost those who believe in him (Heb. 7:25).

II. THE PATTERN FOLLOWED

The principles inherent in Jesus' ministry determined the pattern which he followed. Thereby he brought to bear upon men the saving grace which God offered through him.

1. *The Threefold Ministry of Jesus*

(1) *Preaching, teaching, and healing.*—This pattern is readily discernible in Mark 1. Following his temptation experience, "Jesus came into Galilee, preaching the gospel of the kingdom of God" (Mark 1:14). Shortly thereafter, "They

went into Capernaum; and straightway on the sabbath day he entered into the synagogue, and taught" (v. 21). Later that same day he healed many (vv. 29-34).

Jesus came to save man in his entirety. Whether in preaching, teaching, or healing, his approach was directed toward revealing himself as the power of God unto salvation.

Every phase of Christian work should be to that end. If it cannot so justify itself, it has no place in the program of a Christian, a church, or a denomination. Preachers should preach for a verdict. Richard Baxter said,

> I preached as never sure to preach again,
> And as a dying man to dying men.

The teacher should visit and teach for a verdict. The healing ministry of Christian hospitals should be but a means to an end.

An African chief went to a mission hospital, where he was treated for an illness. Upon being cured, he said, "If your God can heal my body, maybe he can heal my soul." Thus was opened the way for the word of life.

(2) *The primacy of teaching.*—Jesus placed his major emphasis upon teaching. But to him, teaching was not merely the recitation of facts. He taught people, not things.

A seminary professor asked the difference between teaching and preaching. The class concluded that teaching that does not preach is not teaching. Likewise, preaching that does not teach is not preaching. This conclusion was based upon the idea that teaching is designed to instruct the mind, while preaching is intended to move the will to action based upon the thing taught. Jesus did both of these things in his teaching. He instructed the mind and he challenged the will.

Our Lord varied the method of his teaching. Sometimes it was by precept, at others by example. It might be in parables, through nature study, or by questions and answers. He often used the project method of teaching. At times he taught on the basis of events of the moment. He found truth in Scripture and in secular history. Jesus was not a slave to any one method.

A conference leader asked, "What is the worst method of teaching?" He answered his own question: "The worst method of teaching is the one you use all the time."

(3) *The topics of teaching.*—The topics of Jesus' teaching were varied but vital. He taught about God (Matt. 11:27; Luke 11:13; John 4:21, 24). He taught about man (Luke 2:24-25; 13:3; John 3:3). He revealed the Messiah, and identified himself in that role (Matt. 16:13-20; John 4:25-26; 6:35; 8:7, 11-12; 14:6).

Our Lord dealt with such subjects as love (John 3:16), prayer (Matt. 6:9 ff.), sin (Matt. 5:27 ff.), conviction (John 16:8 ff.), repentance (Luke 13:1 ff.), faith (John 3:18), and eternal life (John 3:15-18). He taught at length about heaven (Matt. 5:12; 6:20; Luke 10:20; John 14:1-3), and hell (Matt. 5:22, 29-30; 23:33; Mark 9:43-48). He revealed his passion (Matt. 17:22-23), death, and resurrection (Luke 24:44-46). He told of his return and the final judgment (Matt. 24-25). Jesus instructed his disciples as to their responsibility in declaring the gospel to a lost world (Matt. 28:19-20; Luke 24:46-49; John 20:21).

In his teaching Jesus ran the entire gamut of human need and emotion. Anyone who aspires to teach for him should study his methods, content, and purpose. An examination of modern methods of teaching reveals that Jesus used all of them. After two thousand years, man, by mental development through trial and error, has only approximated in part that which was inherent in Jesus' methods of instruction.

2. *Jesus Seeking the Lost*

Of himself Jesus said, "For the Son of man is come to seek and to save that which was lost" (Luke 19:10). By parable (Luke 15) and allegory (John 10:7 ff.) he set forth this central purpose of his ministry. In every place and in every way he demonstrated this as the very purpose of his being.

(1) *Some sought Jesus.*—Andrew and John left John the Baptist to seek Jesus (John 1:35 ff.). Nicodemus sought Jesus by night, and found the light of life (John 3:1-12). Lepers came to him, beseeching him to make them clean (Mark 1:40-45). A sinful woman came to him, and went away forgiven (Luke 7:37-50). In his dying moment a thief sought Jesus, and arm in arm walked with him through the gates of glory (Luke 23:42-43). No one ever came to him in faith and went away disappointed.

When hungry souls sought Jesus he was always available and prepared. The words "We would see Jesus" (John 12:21) are written on every heart. They are the unuttered cry of every soul. When they were first spoken by some Greeks, Philip and Andrew relayed their wish to Jesus. In all probability it was granted. Can this be said of present-day disciples?

A young man visited a Sunday school, but later said that he would not return. When asked why, he replied: "I came with a hungry heart. I wanted to see Jesus. But the teacher used his time explaining how his favorite football team won its game the previous day." A woman committed suicide on the front steps of a church in a southern city. It was Sunday night when services should have been in progress. But the church building was dark. She had come seeking help, but none was available. Thereafter the pastor vowed that never again would that church building be closed and dark on Sunday night.

(2) *Some were brought to Jesus.*—Andrew brought his brother, Simon. Philip brought a friend, Nathanael (John 1:41-51). The Samaritan woman brought her entire village (John 4:28-30, 39-42). Four men brought their sick and sinful friend (Mark 2:1 ff.).

Andrew stands in the shadow of his more talented brother.

Yet he is distinctive. In John's Gospel he is mentioned only three times. Yet in each instance, he is pictured as bringing someone to Jesus (1:40; 6:8; 12:22). In fact, according to the record, he was the first person to become a Christian and then seek out another to bring him to Jesus.

Through the years the author has followed the practice of urging people to bring their lost relatives and friends to his study for a talk about Jesus. Usually those brought to him have made professions of faith. This is not due to his skill as a soul-winner. The very fact that they agree to come for the interview means that already their hearts have been prepared, their wills are ready to yield to Christ.

(3) *Others Jesus sought.*—Jesus did not end his soul-winning efforts with those who came seeking him or who were brought to him. He came to seek and to save those who were lost. Early in his ministry this truth is affirmed. "The day following Jesus would go forth into Galilee, and findeth Philip, and saith unto him, Follow me" (John 1:43). The word "findeth" suggests a search on the part of Jesus.

In Luke 15 are three parables—the lost sheep, the lost coin, and the lost son. Each story illustrates the seeking ministry of Jesus. A shepherd leaves ninety-nine sheep which were safely in the fold, to find one sheep that was lost. A woman lights a candle, and seeks "diligently" until she finds one lost coin. A father's love reaches out across the miles, seeking to bring his lost son home.

Jesus also sought the lost through his followers. On two different occasions Jesus sent them forth on definitely evangelistic missions (the twelve, Mark 6:7 ff.; the seventy, Luke 10:1 ff.). In the case of the seventy it is specifically stated that he sent them "before his face into every city and place, whither he himself would come" (Luke 10:1). Like John the Baptist, they were to be forerunners preparing the way for him.

No person who aspires to be a soul-winner can be content

to wait for others either to come or to be brought to him. If he would follow the example of Jesus, he must be actively engaged in seeking the lost. Too often evangelism is centered in the church building. In the average preaching service, the number of unsaved who are present is small indeed. A Sunday school teacher boasted to her pastor that she had no unsaved pupils in her class. Instead, she should have been disturbed, because she had not sought to enrol lost people whom she might win.

It is a tried and true statement that "when we go, they come." But they will hardly come of their own accord. In this modern world there are too many things which allure them elsewhere. If they come, they must be sought.

This seeking is not the duty of the pastor alone. Through the Sunday school, the Training Union, and other church activities, the pastor, like Jesus, must enlarge his ministry by seeking through others. In so doing he must set the example.

(4) *Jesus' wayside ministry.*—One of the most effective methods employed by Jesus in evangelism was his wayside ministry. This refers to his chance meetings with those who needed his ministry. It is seen in the cases of Bartimaeus (Mark 10:46-52), the Gadarene demoniac (Luke 8:26-39), the man blind from birth (John 9:1 ff.), and the woman taken in adultery (John 8:1 ff.). Other such instances abound.

Perhaps the most outstanding of these examples is Jesus' meeting with the woman in Samaria (John 4:3 ff.). Here the master soul-winner is seen at work. It will be well to study him. Note the progress of this interview.

First, Jesus made a point of contact through a common interest. "Jesus saith unto her, Give me to drink" (John 4:7).

Second, the woman scorned Jesus. "How is it that thou, being a Jew, askest drink of me, which am a woman of Samaria? for the Jews have no dealings with the Samaritans" (v. 9).

Third, Jesus gained her interest. "The woman saith unto him, Sir, give me this water, that I thirst not, neither come hither to draw" (v. 15).

Fourth, Jesus compelled her respect. "The woman saith unto him, Sir, I perceive that thou art a prophet" (v. 19).

Fifth, he led her to a timid acceptance of him. "Come, see a man, which told me all things that ever I did: is not this the Christ?" In the original language this question indicates that she is convinced herself, but she puts the question in hesitant form to avoid opposition.

Sixth, she openly declares Jesus to be "indeed the Christ, the Saviour of the world" (v. 42). While not definitely stated, it is evident that she joined the others in this confession.

Every Christian can have similar experiences, if he is alert to seize upon them. In the office, on the street, on the golf course, everywhere, these opportunities abound.

An English preacher, meeting someone on the street, might talk of politics, the weather, or some other subject of passing interest. But always before they parted, the preacher would say, "Now, just a word about the Lord Jesus."

3. Jesus Developing the Saved

Jesus' method in evangelism did not end with conversion. He persevered in the development of those whom he had won.

(1) *Enlistment.*—After their conversion he called Simon, Andrew, James, and John from their nets (Mark 1:17). He called Matthew from his custom house (Matt. 9:9). "He ordained twelve, that they should be with him, and that he might send them forth to preach" (Mark 3:14 ff.). To the Gadarene demoniac he said, "Return to thine own house, and shew how great things God hath done unto thee" (Luke 8:39). To the seventy he said, "The harvest truly is great, but the labourers are few: pray ye therefore the Lord of

the harvest, that he would send forth labourers into his harvest" (Luke 10:2).

The average church fails at this point. When a person is won to Christ, his heart is on fire. He is ready and eager to do God's full will. But no one offers him a means whereby it may be done. He is not taught the stewardship either of life or of substance. He is not enlisted for service. Soon he joins the vast church "army of the unemployed." His ardor cools, and, while his soul is saved, his life largely is lost to God. Most of this tragic condition is explained by the words of the men idle in the market place: "Because no man hath hired us" (Matt. 20:7).

(2) *Teaching.*—Jesus not only enlisted workers. He taught them. The Sermon on the Mount is simply Jesus' lesson as to the attitudes and conduct which should characterize every citizen of God's kingdom (Matt. 5-7). His great group of parables (Mark 4:1-34 and parallels in Matthew and Luke) are "his doctrine" regarding the kingdom of God. Jesus' discourse on the Mount of Olives (Matt. 24-25) is his lesson to the twelve regarding contemporary history, his second advent, and the final judgment (Matt. 24:3). With patience and repetition Jesus never ceased to teach his disciples, until he was taken up into heaven.

To convert a person does not automatically make of him a theologian. A babe must be developed. A pupil must be taught. A Christian must be led into a full understanding of his experience and subsequent responsibility. He must be taught in prayer and Bible study. He needs to understand proper Christian conduct, both positively and negatively. He must be indoctrinated. Space forbids an exhaustive treatment of this theme. But a review of the method of Jesus will enlarge and clarify its concepts.

(2) *Training.*—Jesus not only taught his followers; he also trained and developed their skills. When he sent forth the twelve, he gave them an opportunity to apply what they

had learned. Upon their return they reported "all things, both what they had done, and what they had taught" (Mark 6:30; cf. Luke 10:17). Immediately after the return of the twelve Jesus took them apart for a period of six months. Among other reasons for this, certainly one was that he might concentrate upon teaching and training them. The cross was only one year away, and they must be ready to assume their enlarged ministry. They were enthusiastic, slow pupils, but Jesus was a patient, skilful teacher.

Public school systems have supervised teaching. Should churches have less? Industry thrives on on-the-job training. Why not churches? Insurance companies assign a new salesman to an experienced one. Why not do this in soul-winning?

A technological school follows a most practical system. Its students spend one half of the school year in classes. The other half they spend in practical industry, applying what they have learned. This was the method of Jesus. It should be the program of his churches.

III. THE GOAL ENVISIONED

To Jesus this was no idle exercise. It was to the end that God's will might be done on earth as it is in heaven.

Someone asked a ditch digger, "Why do you dig this ditch?" He replied, "I dig the ditch to make the money to buy the bread to give me the strength to dig the ditch." No purpose or goal was in his activity. It was not so with Jesus.

1. *The Intermediate Conquest*

Upon hearing the report of the seventy, Jesus said, "I beheld Satan as lightning fall from heaven" (Luke 10:18). Here was the beginning of the end for Satan. The victory is not complete, but it has begun. And it was through the intermediate agency of those who had avowed their faith in Jesus. Through their faithfulness and sacrifice the battle continues to a successful conclusion.

2. *The Great Commission*

Having finished his redemptive work, Jesus placed full responsibility upon his disciples and those who should follow them (Matt. 28:19-20).

This is affirmed by Jesus' words in Matthew 16:19: "And I will give unto thee the keys of the kingdom of heaven: and whatsoever thou shalt bind on earth shall be bound in heaven: and whatsoever thou shalt loose on earth shall be loosed in heaven." The "keys of the kingdom" are the gospel by which the gates of heaven are to be opened or kept shut to all man. The words "shall be bound" and "shall be loosed" literally read "shall have been bound," and "shall have been loosed." Heaven has already decreed that by Christian people either binding or loosing the gospel, men will be lost or saved thereby.

3. *The Condition and Result*

The "blessed hope" of the Christian is the return of the Lord. Only one definite condition did Jesus give for this event. "And this gospel of the kingdom shall be preached in all the world for a witness unto all nations; and then shall the end come" (Matt. 24:14).

At the second advent the result will be judgment (Matt. 25:31-36). Those who are "in Christ" will be saved. All others will be lost. The judgment will be to declare the condition which already exists in every soul. That condition is being determined now!

FOR DISCUSSION AND CLASSWORK

1. What is meant by the attributes of God? Name his moral attributes. See *Fundamentals of Our Faith*, by Herschel H. Hobbs, chapter on "God," for his natural attributes.
2. What is involved in the depravity of man? Are all people equally depraved in God's sight?
3. Why did Jesus major on teaching? In what way are preaching and teaching related?
4. Let the class members relate incidents of their own wayside ministry.
5. Can a priest forgive sin? What did Jesus mean by "binding" and "loosing?"

CHAPTER 6 OUTLINE

I. THE PRINCIPLES ASSUMED

   1. The Final Revelation of God
   2. The Centrality of Jesus Christ
   3. The Power of the Holy Spirit
   4. The Universal Need for Salvation
   5. The Responsibility of the Redeemed

II. THE PATTERN ACTIVATED

   1. The Responsibility Accepted
   2. The Message Defined
   3. The Pattern Formulated
   4. The Program Followed

III. THE RESULTS ATTESTED

   1. The Emphasis upon Results
   2. A Vitalized People

6

The New Testament Principles
and Pattern

[*In the Witness of the Churches*]

WHEN God completed his redemptive work through his Son, he entrusted the proclamation of it to Jesus' disciples rather than to angels. Other than Jesus, only sinners saved by grace can preach properly the gospel of grace.

The effectiveness of that preaching is by the power of God. "But we have this treasure in earthen vessels, that the excellency of the power may be of God, and not of us" (2 Cor. 4:7).

Through this power the first-century Christians founded and followed a program of evangelism whose success still astounds students of religion. The Christian gospel so challenged the pagan Roman Empire that in less than three centuries the emperor, largely for political reasons, proclaimed Christianity to be the official religion.

The Acts and the Epistles record the beginnings of the evangelistic efforts of the churches and the disciples in which are found the applied principles and resultant pattern for New Testament evangelism, as revealed by the Holy Spirit. Note, first, the principles assumed; second, the pattern activated; third, the results attested.

I. THE PRINCIPLES ASSUMED

As did Jesus, so the disciples declared certain principles to be true, without stopping to give the proof for them. Upon these principles they built their program of evangelism.

1. *The Final Revelation of God*

In Jesus Christ the first-century Christians found the full and final revelation of God. This is attested in Hebrews 1:1-2: "God, who at sundry times and in divers manners spake in time past unto the fathers by the prophets, hath in these last days spoken unto us by his Son. . . ."

The first-century Christians accepted the lordship of Jesus Christ. On the day of Pentecost Peter declared, "Therefore let all the house of Israel know assuredly, that God hath made that same Jesus, whom ye have crucified, both Lord and Christ" (Acts 2:36; cf. 1 Cor. 2:8; Phil. 2:11).

The early Christians confessed Jesus as Lord (Rom. 10:9). They prayed to him as Lord (Acts 7:59-60). They wrote in his name (1 Cor. 7:10). Their abilities were recognized as gifts from him (1 Cor. 12). They experienced the presence of the Lord (2 Tim. 4:17). Jesus was Lord of the church (Eph. 5:29). To them he was "the blessed and only Potentate, the King of kings, and Lord of lords" (1 Tim. 6:15). Always their only question as to duty was "What shall I do, Lord" (Acts 22:10).

In this light only can first-century evangelism be understood, or twentieth-century evangelism be effective. In no case did the early Christians compromise this belief for the sake of outward uniformity (1 Cor. 12:3). Forbidden to preach in his name, they answered: "Whether it be right in the sight of God to hearken unto you more than unto God, judge ye. For we cannot but speak the things which we have seen and heard" (Acts 4:19-20). Multitudes of Christians went to their death saying, "Jesus is Lord," rather than to confess, "Caesar is Lord."

These same "principalities and powers" exist today. Some pulpits mouth empty phrases in their denial of the lordship of Christ. Some councils and tribunals seek to tell how and

where the gospel shall be preached. The constant encroachments of government tend to lull the Christian forces into
looking to it for the solution of the world's ills. But God has
spoken through his Son. He has no other word.

2. The Centrality of Jesus Christ

The first-century Christians regarded Jesus Christ, crucified, buried, risen, and seen alive by them, as central in their
gospel message (1 Cor. 15:3 ff.). Shortly after Pentecost, to
the Sanhedrin itself Peter said, "By the name of Jesus Christ
of Nazareth, whom ye crucified, whom God raised from the
dead, even by him doth this man stand here before you
whole . . . neither is there salvation in any other: for there
is none other name under heaven given among men, whereby
we must be saved" (Acts 4:10-12). Paul, by the Holy Spirit,
said, "For there is one God, and one mediator between God
and men, the man Christ Jesus, who gave himself a ransom
for all" (1 Tim. 2:5-6).

There is no need to multiply quotations. But there is need
for a reminder that the gospel has not changed.

During a series of revivals in Korea many accepted Christ
to the joy of missionaries, pastors, and people. They were
amazed at the simplicity of the sermons. One pastor said of
the president of the Southern Baptist Convention, "Why, all
that he talks about is Jesus!"

3. The Power of the Holy Spirit

The early Christians knew the Holy Spirit as the divine
agent in evangelism (chapter 3). In response to Jesus' ad-
monition, they waited for the Holy Spirit's power. At Pentecost this power was manifested, not only in outward appearance but also in the preaching of the gospel and in the
saving of three thousand souls (Acts 2:1-41). In danger they
found assurance in this power (Acts 4:31). By him doors
were opened, not only jail doors (Acts 5:19), but the doors

to men's hearts (Acts 8:36 ff.), and of entire continents (Acts 13:2; 16:6 ff.). In every sense they realized that all that they did, said, and wrote was by the power of the Holy Spirit.

If one were asked to put his finger upon the greatest need in present-day evangelism, he would not have far to look. It is the power of the Holy Spirit in its programs and schemes. The author discussed a proposed program with the chairman of deacons. The latter said: "Yes, programs are important. But they are not enough. Our church must have a new spirit to match its new program." And that new "spirit" must be the Holy Spirit possessing and using its members in his work.

In a certain church the pastor was not in the pulpit at the appointed hour of the service. When he continued to be absent, a deacon, thinking that he might be ill, went to the pastor's study to investigate. Approaching the door he heard the pastor saying over and over, "I will not go without you." Hesitating to intrude, the deacon waited. Finally, believing that the pastor had forgotten the time, the deacon dared to open the door. He found the pastor on his knees, agonizing in prayer for the Spirit's power.

4. The Universal Need for Salvation

The first-century Christians recognized that all men are lost and need a Saviour. This was true of Jews gathered from every part of the Roman Empire (Acts 2:9-11); half-Jews, or Samaritans (Acts 8:5); a Jewish proselyte (Acts 8:27 ff.); a Roman God-fearer (Acts 10); and pagan philosophers (Acts 17:16 ff.). These early evangels did not regard a man's sincerity as the sole criteria of the validity of his religion. All had sinned, and come short of the glory of God (Rom. 3:23).

If a man went from door to door selling vacuum cleaners, he would find some who did not need one. Some might already own one, but a successful salesman could not so assume without inquiry. Neither can any man aspiring to be a soul-winner so assume. Nor can he excuse himself from trying, simply because some are not interested or are satisfied with less than the best. All who are outside of Christ are his responsibility.

5. *The Responsibility of the Redeemed*

On Olivet Jesus said, "Ye shall be witnesses unto me both in Jerusalem, and in all Judaea, and in Samaria, and unto the uttermost part of the earth" (Acts 1:8). With these words echoing in their hearts, the one hundred and twenty returned to Jerusalem. This became the theme of their lives. The subsequent account in Acts, and in the Epistles, is an enlarged commentary upon this command of Jesus. It is the secret of their success in evangelism.

II. The Pattern Activated

On the basis of these principles a definite pattern of evangelism was formed. Under the guidance of the Holy Spirit, it was wrought out in the hot fires of evangelistic fervor and upon the anvil of circumstances. But always it was true to the principles which formed its blueprint.

1. *The Responsibility Accepted*

This was true whether it involved preaching the gospel in Jerusalem (Acts 2:1 ff.), in Asia Minor (Acts 13:2), or in breaking the traditional ties to launch a crusade in Europe (Acts 16:10). The early Christians suffered violence (Acts 13:19-21), overcame prejudices (Acts 10:14), crossed boundaries (Acts 17:1 ff.), and endured every kind of indignity (Acts 16:22; 17:32) for the privilege of being used by God in his redemptive mission. The Holy Spirit provided guidance and power; and the human element was equal to its task.

A pastor, with one of his trusted laymen, went over a plan for enlisting the men of the church in evangelism. Finally, the layman remarked: "Pastor, the plan is good. It has but one weakness, the human element. Will they do it?" That is the question. God has commanded, the Holy Spirit has provided, but will they do it?

2. The Message Defined

The message of the early evangelists had to be defined. What should they preach and teach? Upon what elements of the gospel should the emphasis be placed? The answer was not long in coming. Speaking by the Holy Spirit Peter declared, "Jesus of Nazareth, a man approved of God among you by miracles and wonders and signs, . . . him, being delivered by the determinate counsel and foreknowledge of God, ye have taken, and by wicked hands have crucified and slain: whom God hath raised up" (Acts 2:22-24). Is there a better summation of the gospel than that?

Here are the humanity of Jesus, God's approval, Jesus' power, man's wickedness, God's redemptive purpose, Jesus' death and resurrection, and God's judgment upon sin and death. Add to these God's promise of Jesus' ultimate victory at his second advent (Acts 2:34-35), the lordship of Christ, and his saviourhood (Acts 2:36). No wonder Peter's hearers were convicted of sin and induced to cry for mercy! This body of truth became the gospel of the early Christians, and God honored it.

This gospel had to be kept pure. Soon the Judaizers came with their gospel of faith plus works, in contrast to the gospel of grace. The first general conference in Christian history was convened in an effort to silence this heresy (Acts 15). But the decision of the conference, guided by the Holy Spirit (Acts 15:28), was unheeded by these heretics. From the blazing pen of Paul comes Galatians, and later Romans, to refute their teachings. In greater or lesser degree, every epistle in the New Testament was designed toward keeping the gospel pure. Misunderstanding about the second coming of Christ occasioned the Thessalonian letters. Questions raised by Gnostic philosophers about the person of Christ evoked Colossians and the epistles of John. Doubts as to the bodily resurrection produced 1 Corinthians 15.

The point is that these early Christians had a gospel. They preached and taught it without compromise. Those who did otherwise were neither condoned nor tolerated. Here is Paul's attitude. "But though we, or an angel from heaven, preach any other gospel unto you than that which we have preached unto you, let him be accursed. For do I now persuade men, or God? or do I seek to please men? for if I yet pleased men, I should not be the servant of Christ" (Gal. 1:8, 10; cf. 1 John 4:2-3; 2 John 7).

The degree that Christianity tones down its message marks the degree of its failure in evangelism. If heresy is taught in Christian colleges and seminaries, it will soon be preached from the pulpits. It will subsequently find its way into church literature and be taught in church schools. The result will be a dearth in evangelism. Twentieth-century Christianity should take the example of its first-century forebears.

3. The Pattern Formulated

A study of Acts reveals a definite pattern which was followed by the early Christians in evangelism.

(1) *Every Christian a witness.*—When Peter preached at Pentecost, the other one hundred and nineteen were not silent. This is affirmed in Acts 2:6-7: "Every man heard *them* speak in his own language. And they were all amazed and marvelled, saying one to another, Behold, *are not all these which speak Galilaeans?*" (author's italics). They witnessed as Peter preached. When persecution came, "therefore they that were scattered abroad went every where preaching the word" (Acts 8:4). The apostles did not leave Jerusalem at this time (Acts 8:1). Stephen, a deacon, due to his fervent preaching, became the first Christian martyr. Philip, a dea-

con, carried the gospel to Samaria and elsewhere. Acquila and Priscilla, "lay" people, instructed Apollos in the gospel.

The responsibility for witnessing was not confined to any one group or order. Every Christian was endowed with gifts which he was to use for the Lord (1 Cor. 12). Satan won a major battle when he caused Christian people to be separated into clergy and laity. The end result is the popular idea that pastors only are to witness for Christ. Evangelism will never make its intended impact upon sin until it be recognized as "every Christian's job."

Often a pastor is asked by one of his flock, "How is your church getting along?" or "How is your revival doing?" It is the questioner's church and revival, if only he will make it so.

(2) *The planned ministry.*—The early churches also had a planned ministry. It is seen in Acts 6 where the church set apart seven men to assist the apostles in their ministry. As a result "the word of God increased; and the number of disciples multiplied in Jerusalem greatly; and a great company of the priests were obedient to the faith" (Acts 6:7).

A revival broke out in Antioch, and Barnabas was called to direct it. So greatly did it flourish that he sought Saul of Tarsus to assist him (Acts 11:19-26). Definite missionary planning is seen in the Antioch church's response to the Holy Spirit in setting apart Barnabas and Saul as missionaries (Acts 13:1 ff.). That they regarded themselves as missionaries from this church is seen in their report to it (Acts 14:27-28).

In addition to their independent work, the churches acted in co-operation. A doctrinal crisis brought the churches of Antioch and Jerusalem together in conference (Acts 15; Gal. 2). Here the leaders conferred, and later reported to the Jerusalem congregation for a corporate decision (Acts 15:6 ff., 12 ff.). Persecution created an economic crisis in Palestine. The churches throughout the Roman Empire co-operated in coming to the rescue (1 Cor. 16:1-4; 2 Cor. 8-9).

The Holy Spirit is not averse to plans and programs. Indeed, he guides in their making and desires to indwell them. If techniques seem to stifle the Spirit, it is the fault of the performers and not of the plans. Furthermore, churches may well co-operate with one another in evangelism and other worthy causes. The increasing results of simultaneous evangelistic crusades attest this truth. New Testament Christians are an independent people, but they express their independence through voluntary co-operation.

(3) *The wayside ministry.*—But first-century Christians were not dependent altogether upon planned events. Wherever they went, they seized upon every opportunity to tell the gospel story (cf. Acts 2-4; 6:8-40). Paul serves as a good example. Arrested, he preached to a mob which wanted to lynch him (Acts 22). Brought before the tribunal of governors and kings, he preached (Acts 24:10 ff.; 26). Chained to a Roman soldier, he preached (Phil. 1:12-13).

The average Christian misses many such opportunities to witness. Perhaps they are not so dramatic but they are nevertheless real. A group of women in a Sunday school class said they did not know a single unsaved person. What a tragedy! Yet they moved in a broad circle of society which doubtless contained many. It is the Christian's duty to know unsaved people, and to try to win them to Christ. How many would know what to say if such an opportunity presented itself? A Christian man happened upon the scene of an accident, where a dying man begged for someone to tell him how to be saved. Later the Christian wept because he did not know what to say.

4. *The Program Followed*

The program of evangelism in the early churches is quite clear.

(1) *Areas defined.*—Actually the areas included in first-century evangelism included Jerusalem, Judea, Samaria, and

"unto the uttermost part of the earth" (Acts 1:8; cf. Rom. 15:15-20).

This pattern might well serve as an outline of Acts. From Jerusalem the gospel spread throughout Palestine. The first missionary journey of Barnabas and Saul reached Cyprus and certain areas of Asia Minor (Acts 13:4, 14-26). In subsequent missions Paul went through Asia Minor, and thence to Europe (Acts 16:6-12). Hereafter, his efforts carried him to Athens, Philippi, Thessalonica, Berea, Corinth, Ephesus, and finally to Rome. From his pastoral epistles (1 and 2 Tim.; Titus) it is inferred that he later went to Spain, the "uttermost" part of the Roman Empire. Paul's stated desire was to preach the gospel in virgin territory (Rom. 15:18-20). Early Christian tradition relates that the other apostles went to various parts of the world. This may or may not be true. But at least one division of responsibility is indicated in Galatians 2:7-9, Paul to the Gentiles and Peter to the Jews.

This is not to be interpreted in terms of a comity agreement. For both declared the gospel to Jews and Gentiles as the opportunity presented itself (Acts 10; 14:1 ff.).

Wherever lost people are found, there is the Christian's field of evangelism. The drawing of imaginary boundaries is the work of man, not of God. A new pastor received a call from a fellow pastor. His purpose was to explain boundaries beyond which each should not go. The former replied: "The field is the world. There are people in each 'area' which one can win better than the other. If so, they are our responsibilities." Of course, in all such relationships, Christian courtesy and ethics should prevail. Generally speaking, a church will have a field which is determined by community interests and needs. However, no Christian witness should be considered "off bounds" if he crosses the other side of the street which is generally understood to comprise a line of separation between church fields. Christian people are to witness wherever they are—in the shop, in the office, the club, or wherever they mingle with people.

(2) *Churches established.*—Wherever the witnesses went, they established churches (cf. Acts 14:23; 16:5). Since there were no church buildings, these churches met in school buildings (Acts 19:9), private homes (Acts 18:7; cf. Philemon 2), or any place where people might be gathered (Acts 20:7 ff.). These became little "colonies of heaven" in a pagan world (Phil. 3:20). They were sounding boards for the gospel (1 Thess. 1:8). Paul's strategy was to establish churches in metropolitan centers, which, in turn, reached out to found other churches in their respective vicinities (cf. Colossae and Laodicea).

The effectiveness of evangelism is enhanced thereby. A pastor argued for busses to take people from unchurched areas to his church. A mission Sunday school would have been far more effective, had he taken the long look. A report indicated that all churches showing a decided gain in Sunday school enrolment were in new communities. This is true in most cases.

(3) *Churches strengthened.*—Nor were these churches or converts left to themselves. Those who were responsible carried out a program of strengthening them. Leaders were chosen and set apart for their ministry (Acts 14:21-23). The churches were strengthened in their faith (Acts 16:4-5). Problems, both practical and doctrinal, were dealt with (Galatians, Corinthian and Thessalonian letters, Philippians, Colossians, and others). Churches were admonished against evil and idleness (Rev. 2-3). They were challenged to fulfil their part in God's world mission (Hebrews). Converts were enlisted, developed, and trained (1 Cor. 12-14; Heb. 10:22-25; 12:12-17). All of this evangelistic work was carried on under democratic procedures.

A minister who held a place of leadership in another Christian group expressed to the author his amazement at the co-operation shown between churches and conventions of the latter's denomination. He asked, "Is pressure exerted upon you to do so?" The author replied that in more than thirty years in the pastorate he had known no pressure, except the desire to co-operate with his brethren in a common cause for Christ. That can be possible only through churches developed in the faith, and through a program worthy of eliciting co-operation. Evangelism is at its center.

III. The Results Attested

The supreme test of any program is the results obtained.

1. *The Emphasis upon Results*

One has but to read the book of Acts to see that these early Christians placed emphasis upon results. Futhermore, they reported the results obtained (Acts 14:27). Statistics to them were not dead figures, but the records of spiritual fruit.

The following citations are evidence of this fact: Acts 2:41; 4:4; 6:7; 8:12, 36; 10:44-48; 11:21, 24; 12:24; 13:48; 14:27; 17:11-12, 34. Note the numbers: "three thousand souls," "about five thousand," "the number of the disciples multiplied," "a great number believed," "much people was added unto the Lord," and "the word of God grew and multiplied."

It has been the author's observation that those who deplore the emphasis upon results have little to report. A pastor said, "I long for the day when Baptists will graduate from the book of 'numbers.'" Such a wish cannot be justified by the Bible.

A church reported its revival to the paper: "There were no additions, but the church was greatly revived." Is this a contradiction of terms? If Christian people are truly revived, souls will be saved as a result. Imagine a salesman reporting to his manager, "I had a very successful trip, but I have no sales to report." What must the "Sales Manager" of the churches think, when they do likewise?

2. A *Vitalized People*

The first-century churches had problems. But they were the problems of a vitalized people. Vibrant children may at times break the parent's heart. Dead children create no problems, except those of grief and interment. Of the church at Laodicea Jesus said: "I know thy works, that thou art neither cold nor hot: I would thou wert cold or hot. So then because thou art lukewarm, and neither cold nor hot, I will spue thee out of my mouth" (Rev. 3:15-16). Such a church is even nauseating to the Lord!

But the overall teaching of Acts and the Epistles is that with infinite patience the Holy Spirit deals with problem churches which are alive unto him. And to them he says, "Be ye steadfast, unmoveable, always abounding in the work of the Lord, forasmuch as ye know that your labour is not in vain in the Lord" (1 Cor. 15:58).

FOR DISCUSSION AND CLASSWORK

1. What is meant by the "lordship of Christ"?
2. Does the Holy Spirit work with Christians today as in the first century? How?
3. Are methods a help or a hindrance in evangelism?
4. Should the churches compromise the gospel on behalf of outward unity with other denominations?
5. Is the Southern Baptist Simultaneous Evangelistic Crusade in keeping with New Testament methods?

CHAPTER 7 OUTLINE

I. THE FIELD OF RELIGIOUS EDUCATION
   1. The Biblical Basis of Religious Education
   2. Religious Education Defined
   3. Religious Education Described

II. RELIGIOUS EDUCATION IN WINNING THE LOST
   1. The Responsibility of Every Unit
   2. The Focal Point of the Sunday School

III. RELIGIOUS EDUCATION IN DEVELOPING THE SAVED
   1. The Goal of New Testament Evangelism
   2. The Fellowship in Responsibility
   3. The Means to an End

7

The Relation of Religious Education
to Evangelism

AT THE OUTSET of this chapter it is well to recall the larger concept of evangelism. It involves not only winning the lost to Christ. It also includes the growth, development, and enlistment of those who are won. To neglect any one of these is to miss the mark in evangelism.

This broad concept of evangelism is inherent in the entire scope of present-day religious education. It is suggested that this be kept in mind in considering first, the field of religious education; second, religious education in winning the lost; third, religious education in developing the saved.

I. THE FIELD OF RELIGIOUS EDUCATION

The concern here is not with respect to the work done by Christian colleges and seminaries. Instead, it is confined to the work of churches.

1. *The Biblical Basis of Religious Education*

This basis is found in the Great Commission itself (Matt. 28:19-20). There the emphasis is placed upon teaching. "Make disciples" or "teach all nations," "baptizing them," and "teaching them to observe all things whatsoever I have commanded you." These are the words of Jesus himself (cf. Deut. 31:12). They express the purpose, method, and goal of religious education. Jesus made them so, and he commanded his people to do likewise.

2. Religious Education Defined

For this study religious education may be defined very simply. It is the organized effort through which a church endeavors to enlist, teach, and preach for the purpose of winning unsaved people to Christ, and to develop Christian people in their growth in grace, knowledge, and service for Christ. In this sense it is synonymous with evangelism.

Someone asked, "Does not evangelism end with conversion?" The answer is, "Yes, but which end?" This serves to indicate that evangelism does not end with regeneration. It begins with the first contact made with a lost person. It does not end until that person comes into the fulness of the stature of Christ.

3. Religious Education Described

It is easier to describe religious education than to define it. In a Southern Baptist church the following program is designed to meet all of a person's spiritual needs. For the immediate purpose, it is necessary only to mention briefly its various phases.

The Sunday school is the church enlisting people of all ages for the dual purpose of Bible teaching and soul-winning (Matt. 11:28-30). The Training Union primarily is the church enlisting and training those who have been won to Christ. The Woman's Missionary Union is the church guiding the women and children in the study and practice of missions, and in the stewardship relating to missions (Luke 8:3). The Brotherhood is the church enlisting and developing its men and boys in undergirding the entire program of the church (Luke 10:1 ff.). Group training is utilized by the church in extended study, through the Church Study Course for Teaching and Training, to develop its membership in Bible study, doctrine, and the various themes relating to the Christian life.

A graded music program creates a taste for good religious music, enhances worship, instructs all ages in musical appreciation and service, and trains those who are talented in music for a more effective use of their gifts (Eph. 5:19). The church library provides good reading material and encourages its proper use (1 Tim. 4:13). Visual aids are used to supplement and enrich the entire teaching and training program (Matt. 3:13 ff.; 13:3; 26:26-28). Through this ministry truth comes alive to teach through the eyes and the imagination. The church also has a guided program of Christian recreation, developing the physical, spiritual, and social elements of the individuals and the group (1 Cor. 9:24-27).

The church council, composed of the elected heads of all organizations, serves to co-ordinate all activities. Through its ministry an orderly procedure and a maximum efficiency are obtained (Acts 15; 1 Cor. 12:27; 14:33). In one church a list was made of the specific functions which comprised its program of religious education. There were fifty of them. Such a program will result in bedlam without a proper co-ordination.

The pulpit ministry of the churches is mentioned last, not because it is of the least but of the greatest importance (2 Tim. 4:2). In Baptist churches preaching and worship are central in all of their activities.

It should be noted that no one of the aforementioned phases of religious education is a unit unto itself. All are interrelated to perform one complete function, the building up of the body of Christ (cf. 1 Cor. 12:14; cf. 12:4-14:40).

If it seems that this program is mechanical, remember that a true church is not an organization, nor a series of organizations bound together in outward conformity. It is an organism wherein abides life. Its very breath is the Holy Spirit who indwells it (1 Cor. 12:4-7).

A machine is composed of many parts, all properly related to one another, and with specific functions. But it is a dead thing unless power is injected into it. The human body is only a corpse unless it possesses the glow of life. So is a church. Its many facets of activity are designed to give it a well-rounded ministry. But apart from the Holy Spirit, it has a name that it lives, but it is dead (Rev. 3:1). A church which is responsive to the Holy Spirit is like the church in Philadelphia: "I know thy works: behold, I have set before thee an open door, and no man can shut it" (Rev. 3:8).

II. RELIGIOUS EDUCATION IN WINNING THE LOST

The first responsibility of every church is to win the lost to Christ. If it fails here, it loses its right to exist. This Jesus affirms in Revelation 2:4-5.

1. *The Responsibility of Every Unit*

Soul-winning is the responsibility of every organization within a church. The primary function of a given unit may lie in some other area, but it is not exempted from this basic duty. Review the organizations previously listed. There is not one which cannot contribute to the winning of a lost person to Christ. They are all parts of religious education. It has been seen that religious education's first function is to create an atmosphere conducive to an acceptance of Christ as one's Saviour. No soul-winning, no religious education.

The author baptized an entire family. The first contact with the home was through the Christian recreation program. The son was attracted to the church through it. Subsequently the family was enlisted in Sunday school. The result was a family won to Christ.

2. *The Focal Point of the Sunday School*

The focal point in evangelism is the Sunday school. It is estimated that among Southern Baptist churches, approximately 90 per cent of those who are won to Christ come through the Sunday school. Dr. J. N. Barnette said that each year one out of every three enrolled in Sunday school is won, while only one out of more than two hundred not enrolled in Sunday school is reached for Christ. Furthermore, there are many unsaved members of families who have one of their number enrolled in Sunday school. This provides a ready approach to soul-winning efforts through the Sunday school. Thus is seen the importance of a functioning Sunday school in the program of evangelism.

Any pastor who aspires to reach large numbers for Christ will give the time necessary to gain the maximum efficiency from the Sunday school in evangelism. If he does not lead, no one else can.

(1) *Enlargement in Bible study for evangelism.*—This was the theme of a campaign some years ago to reach more people for Christ through the Sunday school. It might well be an abiding one, for it states the purpose and process of this organization in its work.

The slogan of Southern Baptist Sunday schools in 1954 was "A Million More in '54." The previous year Dr. Charles E. Matthews, then the secretary of evangelism for the Southern Baptist Home Mission Board, said to the author: "We must not fail to reach this goal. We have been baptizing people at such a rate that we have about run out of ready prospects. If we fail in this, we shall see a drop in evangelism in the immediate future." Of interest is the fact that in 1954 nearly six hundred thousand people were added to the enrollment of Southern Baptist Sunday schools. In 1955, 416,867 baptisms were reported, the highest in the denomination's history up to that time.

(2) *The methods involved.*—Such an undertaking cannot be left to chance. Its success is the result of carefully laid plans and vigorous efforts on the part of the Sunday school forces. This involves many factors.

a. *Grading.*—The Sunday school is so graded as to implement the purpose of reaching every age. In the younger groups this grading is related not only to age grouping. It relates also to literature and other teaching aids. Its purpose is gradually to introduce the pupil to God, God's ministry to him, and his responsibility to God. In a progressive unfolding of truth, the child is brought to an understanding of the plan of salvation and to a proper response to that plan.

This process is evident to any teacher or parent of Nursery, Beginner, or Primary children. Some years ago the author had this truth brought home to him. As his son progressed through the Primary years, concern was felt as to whether or not he was aware of his need for Christ. While he was in the eight-year Primary department, that awareness blossomed as a flower. It bore fruit about the middle of his first Junior year.

b. *Locating opportunities.*—"Go out into the highways and hedges, and compel them to come in, that my house may be filled" (Luke 14:23).

This is accomplished in many ways. A community or city-wide religious census is the most comprehensive one. Another fruitful source is visitor's cards signed in the various services and activities of the church.

This is especially true in the Sunday school. A welcome in the department assembly repeated in the class can be a word from the Lord. Too often, however, classes tend to let the matter end there. The spiritual welcome must be accompanied by the signing of visitor's cards, or, better still, a classification slip for enrolment. A man went to a Sunday school class with the intention of enrolling. After three Sundays, he gave up and went to another Sunday school. When asked why, he said that no one ever asked him to join the class.

Various civic "welcome" services and utility company records are available through which to locate opportunities. Many newspapers carry a "new residents" column. The chamber of commerce bulletin may prove to be a fertile field in this regard. An alert church will discover many such sources.

But churches must not be content to rely entirely upon these. A pastor followed the practice of watching for moving vans unloading furniture in his community. An informal call at that time may well be the first contact for newcomers to a city. A neighborly visit to these families by church members will prove invaluable. A church may delegate this responsibility to its members in an assigned area. Alertness at the office, factory, or in various social gatherings will prove fruitful.

c. *Assignments of opportunities.*—After opportunities have been located they must be assigned (Acts 10:20). Census cards are not to be filed and forgotten. Many plans are available for the utilization of the information gathered. No plan will work itself. Even an inferior plan is better than none at all. The degree of efficiency will be in direct ratio to the dedication in working whatever plan is adopted.

The organization of the Sunday school is adapted to this purpose. Since Southern Baptist churches grade their Sunday schools on the age basis, the plan is quite simple. Opportunities are assigned to the department into which they naturally fall.

However, before assignment it is wise to make every effort to determine the accuracy of the information contained on each card. A lady called on another. The card said that she was unsaved. When the visitor tried to win her to Christ, she learned that she was already a Christian, and a member of the same church. Naturally, the visit did more harm than good, both to the visited and the visitor. Usually class members do not mind visiting. But they are frustrated and discouraged to find that the card contains the wrong address or incorrect information about the prospect. A worthy group in each Sunday school visitation program is one which makes initial visits to all prospects to check on the accuracy of information before assigning the names to classes. In one church a newcomer-visitation is carried out monthly by a group of women in the church. Henceforth, the names are assigned to responsible groups for further enlistment efforts.

The responsibility for the assignment rests upon the pastor and the general superintendent. Normally this will be done through an associate superintendent charged with this duty. He works through a corresponding officer in each department. In turn, the assignments are passed on to the classes, where they are placed in the hands of responsible officers. It is advisable to keep duplicate records at each level, to insure a proper follow-up. The teacher, through the class organization, is responsible for seeing that the assignments are carried out.

In some instances a teacher will try to do all of this by himself. This method is unfair to him, the class members, and the prospective members. A good teacher can multiply himself many times over by having and using an efficient class organization.

Once the assignments are made, a careful check must be made to insure that they are not forgotten. When Jesus sent his followers forth on an evangelistic mission, they reported to him the results of their efforts (Luke 10:1-17). Here is ample scriptural authority for continuing to do so.

In many instances the number of available opportunities will call for the organization of new departments and/or classes. Whenever a class becomes too large, it loses much of its incentive to seek new members.

One of the greatest Sunday schools in America had an inadequate building. But the pastor was alert to assign every prospect to its proper group. He would often secure a teacher to whom he would give a group of names. He would have a carpenter build a "lean-to" against the side of the building. Then he showed it to the new teacher, and told her to fill it with pupils.

d. *Enlistment of opportunities.*—The foregoing plans are of little or no value unless they result in a vigorous effort to enlist the prospects who have been located and assigned. For this reason every Sunday school needs an intensive program of visitation. Jesus came to seek and to save that which was lost (Luke 19:10; cf. Luke 15). To the Ephesian elders Paul said, "And how I kept back nothing that was profitable unto you, but have shewed you, and have taught you publickly, and from house to house, testifying both to the Jews, and also to the Greeks, repentance toward God, and faith toward our Lord Jesus Christ" (Acts 20:20-21). Need there be any greater examples of house-to-house visitation?

To accomplish this goal, definite plans are necessary. It is well to have a specific time for church-wide visitation. In lieu of this a departmental and class visitation will prove valuable. Without a specified time for this purpose, the results will be far from desirable. A hit-and-miss plan will miss more often than it will hit.

But plans are not enough. They must be accompanied by an incentive and a goal. The true incentive is compassion for the lost. The proper goal is to reach them for Christ. Neither of these can be realized apart from prayer accompanied by effort. No prospect card should be regarded as merely a piece of paper. It represents a lost soul for whom Christ died.

A man read in the paper about the death of another man. Somehow the name seemed familiar. Upon investigating, he found a prospect card in his pocket, long forgotten. It bore the name of the man listed in the obituary column, and he was lost!

One visit usually will not suffice. An insurance salesman said that when he called on a new prospect, he expected to make five visits before he made a sale. He might succeed on the first, but, if not, he continued until he did. Sunday school visitors certainly will do no less. Until a person dies, moves away, joins another Sunday school, or is enlisted, he is both a prospect and a responsibility.

e. *Teaching for a verdict.*—When a lost person is enlisted, the work has just begun. A common weakness in Sunday school work is the attitude that the enrolment of pupils is the goal. It is but a means to an end, the winning of lost people to Christ.

When a person is brought into the Sunday school, there must be something there to bring him back. Even a hearty welcome is not enough. He must experience the presence of God. He must feel an atmosphere charged with love and concern for him. The teaching must be of such a nature as to bring the lost person under conviction for his sins. From the opening note of music leading into the department worship period, through the last word spoken in the class, the purpose is to bring the pupil face to face with Jesus and his claims upon him.

The key person in this phase of Sunday school work is the teacher. Upon him, as upon no other, rests the responsibility of bringing all efforts to a successful conclusion. Therefore, it is imperative that he come to the teaching hour with a lesson from the Word of God. He should be prepared, both intellectually and spiritually. His lesson must be bathed in prayer and taught with concern. Like Paul, he must serve "the Lord with all humility of mind, and with many tears" (Acts 20:19), if not in his eyes, then in his heart. When the hour is through, he should be able to say, "Wherefore I take you to record this day, that I am pure from the blood of all men. For I have not shunned to declare unto you all the counsel of God" (Acts 20:26-27).

This the teacher cannot do if his work is confined to thirty minutes on Sunday morning. Throughout the week, both personally and through his class members, he must teach from house to house, if he teaches properly on Sunday morning. Only then may he teach people, and not merely lessons.

A Sunday school teacher refused to visit his pupils. He gave as the reason: "Why, it would be the height of conceit for me to go around all week, begging people to come to hear me teach on Sunday!" He did not have the least concept of his purpose and responsibility as a teacher.

After the author had been the pastor of a church for a year, a man said to him: "Pastor, I seem to get more out of your sermons now than when you first came. They seem to be more down where I live." The pastor replied: "Well, brother, it has taken me a year to find out where you live. I will be dropping in more often." The teacher must know where, and how, his pupils live, if he is to teach them properly.

f. *Worship service attendance.*—The duty of the class does not end with the class period. As a group it should adjourn into the worship service (Heb. 10:25). In this service it is well that the teacher, especially, endeavor to sit with his lost pupils. The pastor takes up where the teacher left off. When the invitation is given, the teacher finds a golden opportunity to join his appeal to that of the pastor (Acts 2:6-7). Where necessary, he may accompany the saved pupil to the front, as he makes his profession of faith.

After such a service a teacher, with tears of joy, said to her pastor: "This is the teacher's pay. I would not exchange it for all the wealth in the world!"

g. *Beyond baptism.*—The teacher and others are responsible for guiding the newborn Christian into the act of obedience, baptism. Thereafter, the entire program of the Sunday school must be dedicated toward guiding him in growth and development into a useful follower of Christ. The saying may be trite, but it is nevertheless true. The process of evangelism is not complete until the evangelized becomes an evangelist. And a better and better evangelist, until the Lord calls him home!

III. Religious Education in Developing the Saved

If this section of the book seems somewhat repetitious, recall that Jesus found it necessary to repeat his teachings often. An advertising executive was asked what rule governed his company in advertising a product. He said: "We get a spot on the radio or television. There we keep repeating the same thing until the listening public holds up its hands in horror, exclaiming, 'When will they stop saying that?'" "Then," said he, "they are beginning to get it."

1. The Goal of New Testament Evangelism

This goal involves winning lost people to Christ and developing them into fruitful servants of Christ.

Regarding the life that lives forever, Jesus said, "Thou shalt love the Lord thy God with all thy heart, and with all thy soul, and with all thy strength, and with all thy mind; and thy neighbor as thyself" (Luke 10:27; cf. Deut. 6:5). It involves a right relation both to God and man. This is the goal of New Testament evangelism.

2. The Fellowship in Responsibility

When the definitions of a church are reduced to their basic element, a church is a fellowship, wherein its members have all things in common. This is seen in Paul's figure of the church as the body of Christ, with members in particular, and each member having a definite function (1 Cor. 12-14). It is further set forth in Hebrews (10:21-25; 12:12-13) where the fellowship of believers is pictured in their mutual care one for another. The purpose of this fellowship is the development of each member into his full potential for Christ (Eph. 4:11-14).

It takes little imagination to see here the entire program of religious education. Once again the reader will do well to refer to the various facets of this program. Each is designed toward the development of every member into a well-rounded servant of Christ. Under the direction of the pastor this purpose will be accomplished if every organization fulfils its intended function.

3. *The Means to an End*

This means is found particularly in the Training Union. Other organizations may develop certain phases of the Christian's life. But the unique function of the Training Union is the development of the Christian in the full meaning and experience of church membership.

The principal of a high school came to the pastor of a Baptist church, noting that every elected student leader in the school was a Baptist. His inquiry was as to what program a Baptist church had to develop such qualities of leadership which others did not have. It was discovered that every pupil mentioned was an active member of the Training Union.

This development may be regarded in two ways.

(1) *Understanding.*—This involves study designed to inform the mind, and exercises which are conducive to forming certain habits which result in self-development. Through a graded organization, and carefully prepared and graded literature, the person is furnished a guide to wider study in such areas as worship, Bible study, doctrinal instruction, and missionary knowledge. With the emphasis upon Bible reading, he acquires the habit of a daily and systematic reading of his Bible. In the Junior ages he is guided in memorizing many choice passages from the Bible. One emphasis in the Intermediate department is on learning to use the Bible itself.

The Sunday evening program is climaxed by an experience of group worship and evangelism. The editor of a Christian magazine published in the North made a tour of the southern and southwestern states, in order to study the work of the churches. Everywhere he went he found a majority of the churches closed on Sunday night. The major exception was the Baptist churches, in which he found large crowds attending Sunday night services. Searching for the reason for this difference, he concluded that it lay in the Training Union.

(2) *Expression.*—The Training Union is designed to lead every person in the development of his aptitudes through self-expression. In a sense he is not taught; he teaches. And in teaching others he teaches himself. Such activities as reading the Scriptures and leading in prayer are typical of many others involved. The individual learns to stand on his feet and express himself as he delivers his assigned part which he has prepared himself. Through committee work he learns by doing. Through definite projects he learns to participate in the larger aspects of Christian service.

A deacon came to the author and said: "Pastor, I want to pay a tribute to the Training Union. All my life I have been overly timid. It affected me, not only in my church life, but in the business world as well. I used to serve as a secretary in the Sunday school. Then some friends got me in Training Union. At first, I could hardly hold the Bible while reading the Scripture. To pray or speak before the union was unthinkable. Gradually, I gained courage and confidence. Now I am a deacon and an Adult Sunday school superintendent, I endeavor to win souls, and I pray and speak in public. Also I have been advanced to an executive position in my business firm. I still am uneasy, but the Lord, through the Training Union, has enabled me to conquer my fear."

The Training Union is the training ground for a large majority of Christian workers. A certain church was beginning a week of enlargement in its Training Union. The Sunday school superintendent was not attending Training Union. To everyone's surprise he requested that the pastor give him a list of the names of adult couples who were not in Training Union. His stated purpose was that he might organize a new union. When asked as to his sudden change of attitude, he replied: "I made a study of the Sunday school. It revealed to me that most of the teachers and officers were products of the Training Union. I feel that the least I can do is to help train those who work with me in the Sunday school."

The Training Union is so graded as to minister to the growth of every church member. And no one ever reaches beyond the age or degree of development which exempts him from this need.

Many years ago when the Adult unions were first being organized, the educational director of the Broadway Baptist Church, Louisville, Kentucky, announced one Sunday morning that an Adult union would be formed that evening. He invited every adult who felt the need for Christian growth and development to be present. At the appointed hour he waited in the assigned room, wondering if any adults would come. Presently he heard footsteps approaching. When the first person to respond entered the room, it was none other than Dr. John R. Sampey, president of the Southern Baptist Theological Seminary.

FOR DISCUSSION AND CLASSWORK

1. Make a list of religious education activities in your church.
2. Have a student contact the church secretary to determine how many people who were baptized the previous year were members of the Sunday school at the time of conversion.
3. Let another check the lost members in Sunday school to determine how regular they are in attendance in Sunday school and in the worship services.
4. Discuss ways by which the Training Union develops a Christian.

CHAPTER 8 OUTLINE

I. SANCTIFICATION, AN INSTANTANEOUS ACT

    1. The Initial Condition in Sanctification

    2. The Indwelling of the Holy Spirit

    3. The Sacrifice of the Body

II. SANCTIFICATION, A CONTINUING PROCESS

    1. Transformation versus Conformation

    2. Growing in the Will of God

    3. The Work of an Evangelist

III. SANCTIFICATION, AN ULTIMATE GOAL

    1. The End of Sanctification, Glorification

    2. The Degrees of Glorification

    3. The Means to Complete Glorification

    4. The Present Responsibility

8

The Individual and Evangelism

THE PERSON is the focal point in New Testament evangelism. This truth is affirmed in Jesus' evaluation of the individual soul (Mark 8:36). Furthermore, it is seen with regard to the place of the individual in the work of evangelism. Paul so asserts in Ephesians 3:8-11: "*Unto me*, who am less than the least of all saints, is this grace given, that I should preach among the Gentiles [heathen] the unsearchable riches of Christ. . . . according to the eternal purpose which he [God] purposed in Christ Jesus our Lord" (author's italics). In its final analysis the eternal purpose of God waits upon the individual.

This serves to introduce the doctrine of sanctification. Sanctification is synonymous with holiness. In the Old Testament anything which was dedicated to God was regarded as holy or sanctified. In the New Testament these terms are related primarily to persons. All Christians are regarded as saints or sanctified ones (Acts 9:13; Rom. 1:7; 2 Cor. 1:1; Phil. 1:1; Col. 1:2).

The basic meaning in sanctification is not sinlessness, although this idea is present in the word. The primary thought in sanctification is dedication. It was in this sense that Jesus used the word "sanctify" with reference to himself and to his followers (John 17:19).

Santification is the work of the Holy Spirit (2 Thess. 2:13-14; 1 Peter 1:2; Rom. 8:1-17). It is both instantaneous and progressive. The former refers to the act of justification or regeneration (John 3:5). The latter is related to the progressive development of the Christian life as it grows in grace, knowledge, and service in Christ (2 Peter 3:18). The New Testament recognizes no Christian life other than a sanctified one.

The obligation with reference to sanctification is seen in, first, sanctification, an instantaneous act; second, sanctification, a continuing process; third, sanctification, an ultimate goal.

I. Sanctification, an Instantaneous Act

The moment that a person becomes a Christian, he is sanctified to God. In the New Testament three distinct figures are employed to express this thought: new birth (John 3:7); enrolling in school (Matt. 11:28-30); marriage (John 3:29; Matt. 22:2). These figures involve one's "dedication" as a son, a pupil, and a bridegroom, respectively. Beyond the initial experience there follows development within the relationship thus formed. Each may be paralleled in the Christian experience.

1. *The Initial Condition in Sanctification*

This initial experience is conditioned by other experiences on the part of the individual.

(1) *Conviction.*—Before a person can be regenerated, he must recognize that he is a sinner, and is lost from God (Rom. 3:23). This Jesus avowed in Luke 18:13. Unlike the proud Pharisee, the publican regarded himself as the only sinner in the world. He felt himself unworthy even to look at God, much less to stand in his presence. On such an attitude Jesus affirmed his acceptance in God's sight (Luke 18:14).

The clearer one sees God in his holiness, the more unworthy he feels in God's presence (Job 42:5-6; Isa. 6:1-5). A man says to a soul-winner, "I have done nothing for which I need forgiveness." He is not under the convicting power of the Holy Spirit (John 16:8-9). Another person says to him, "I am not worthy to be a Christian" (Luke 15:19). Such a person is not far from the kingdom of God.

(2) *Repentance.*—Conviction must be followed by genuine repentance (Luke 13:3, 5). A convicted person may rebel against God and plunge deeper into sin. Like Judas he may regret only that he got caught (Matt. 27:3-5; the word "repent" here is not the word for genuine repentance. It means human regret without godly sorrow, cf. 2 Cor. 7:10). The word for genuine repentance involves a change of mind, attitude, and heart. The person experiencing this repentance will turn from his sin to God in confession of sin.

In military drill there is a command "To the rear, march!" In executing it a soldier immediately changes his direction. This is the experience of every person who genuinely repents. He turns from Satan to God, from sin to righteousness, and from spiritual death to eternal life.

(3) *Faith.*—This he does as he expresses his faith in Jesus Christ as his Saviour. Realizing his own helpless and undone condition, he turns in faith to Jesus Christ. This Paul affirms in Romans 10:10 when he says, "For with the heart man believeth unto righteousness . . ."

Faith is more than an intellectual assent to the truth of the gospel. It is trust. As a man trusts the weight of his body to a chair, so must he trust his soul to Christ. As he commits his body to an airplane to be transported to his destination, so he commits his soul to Christ unto salvation. As he receives a proffered gift, so he receives Christ as his Saviour (John 1:12).

(4) *Confession.*—The above mentioned quotation from Romans 10:10 is only half the story. Paul added, ". . . and with the mouth confession is made unto salvation." This involves more than the mere saying of words or of joining the church. It includes the outward expression of life (cf. Eph.

2:10; Matt. 3:8; cf. Luke 3:10-14). A man is to prove the genuineness of his faith by his works which result therefrom (James 2:14-26).

In a revival meeting a man responded to the "altar call." The next day he was seen drunk. A cynic pointed him out to the evangelist, saying, "There is one of your converts." To which he replied: "Yes, he looks like some of mine. If the Lord had converted him, he would not be there."

This suggests the weakness of many evangelistic efforts. Too often the emphasis is placed upon joining the church, rather than upon a genuine experience with the Lord through the work of the Holy Spirit. Apart from this latter work, names may be added to the church roll. But souls will not be sanctified to God. Too many churches depend upon gimmicks rather than upon God. Outward schemes may pack the pews, but unless they are bathed in the power of the Holy Spirit they will never edify the body of Christ.

2. *The Indwelling of the Holy Spirit*

Erroneously, by some, sanctification is connected with a "second blessing" or a special filling by the Holy Spirit. According to this view, this infilling is the result of one's efforts in achieving sinless perfection to the point that the Holy Spirit comes upon him as a special blessing.

The New Testament teaches otherwise. An examination of certain passages of Scripture reveals that the Holy Spirit indwells every true believer (John 14:17; Acts 8:15; 9:17; 10:44). There is no specific method by which the Holy Spirit comes into the believer's life. He came through the laying on of the hands of an apostle (Acts 8:15), and by the laying on of the hands of a "layman" (Acts 9:17). He came after men had preached; his coming also interrupted preaching (Acts 10:44). It is idle practice to try to formulate any scheme whereby the Holy Spirit comes into a believer's life.

"The wind [Spirit] bloweth where it [he] listeth [wishes or wills]" (John 3:8).

But to every Christian Paul says, "Know ye not that your body is the temple of the Holy Ghost [Spirit] which is in you, which ye have of God, and ye are not your own? For ye are bought with a price: therefore glorify God in your body, and in your *spirit*, which are God's" (1 Cor. 6:19-20, author's italics). It is not a question as to how much of the Holy Spirit the Christian has, but how much of him the Holy Spirit has.

The fuel tank of an automobile may be filled with gasoline, yet the machine is powerless. For gasoline to do its work it must possess not only the tank, but also the fuel lines, carburetor, spark plugs, cylinders, drive shaft, gears, and wheels. So the Holy Spirit must possess every member and faculty of one's body and life.

3. The Sacrifice of the Body

This truth Paul affirms in Romans 12:1: "I beseech you therefore, brethren, by the mercies of God, that ye present your bodies a living sacrifice, holy, acceptable unto God, which is your reasonable service."

The word "present" translates a word used by the Jewish historian, Josephus, for offering a sacrifice in the Jewish temple. It is used of presenting the child Jesus in the temple (Luke 2:22), and of the Christian presenting (yielding) the members of his body as instruments of righteous service to God (Rom. 6:13; cf. Eph. 5:27; Col. 1:28). So he is to present his body, not as a dead sacrifice, but as a living sacrifice unto God. "To present" (Rom. 12:1), expresses an instantaneous action. The active voice indicates that it is an action done by the Christian himself.

Many Christians, if faced with the necessity, would die for their faith. But how many of them will live for it? At certain seasons of the year many conscientious Christians punish their bodies through denial. In certain areas of the south-western part of the United States and in the Philippine Islands there exists a sect known as Flagellants or Penitentes, self-whippers, who scourge their bodies unmercifully, as a service to God.

The Christian teaching is the opposite of such practices. Instead of denying or destroying the body, it is to be presented to God as sanctified or dedicated to a full development for and in his service (cf. 1 Cor. 6:20).

II. SANCTIFICATION, A CONTINUING PROCESS

But if the act of dedication is an instantaneous one done by the person himself, the process is a continuing one performed by another upon or within the Christian.

1. *Transformation versus Conformation*

In Romans 12:2 Paul enlarges upon his plea in verse 1. "And be not conformed to this world: but be ye transformed by the renewing of your mind . . . !" "This world" means the pattern of thought and life of the age in which these Christians lived. Dr. A. T. Robertson says, "Do not take this age as your fashion plate."[1] The words "be not conformed" and "be ye transformed" are in the present passive imperative form. The present tense suggests a habit of action. The passive voice means that the action is being done to the Christian by another. The imperative mode makes it a command.

The thought is that someone is doing something to the Christian. Either Satan is conforming him to the fashion of the age, or else the Holy Spirit is transforming him into the likeness and service of God in Christ. Paul commands in memorable words that the former be stopped and that the latter be practiced.

This is a timeless exhortation. The greatest weakness of

1. A. T. Robertson, *Word Pictures in the New Testament,* IV (Nashville: Baptist Sunday School Board, 1931), 402.

present-day Christianity is conformed rather than transformed Christians. Too many are concerned with fitting in rather than standing out. Unless the lost person sees something different in the Christian, he has no incentive to change his ways or his condition.

A wife says that she will not put her letter in the church until her husband is saved and joins the church with her. Meanwhile her life is conformed to his sinful ways. Her witness is negative. She is saying by her actions that her Christian experience is not very important. Yet she wonders why her husband makes no decision for Christ.

Paul says that this transformation is to be accomplished "by the renewing of your mind." Dr. Robertson comments tersely, "The new birth, the new mind, the new (*kainos*) man." [2] Its purpose is "that ye may prove what is that good, and acceptable, and perfect, will of God" (Rom. 12:2). Dr. George W. Truett once said, "To know God's will is the greatest knowledge; to find God's will for one's life is the greatest discovery; to do God's will is the greatest achievement."

2. Growing in the Will of God [3]

In the first eleven chapters of Romans Paul expounds doctrine. In chapters 12 to 16 he exhorts to righteous living in the light of that doctrine. Chapters 12 to 14 deal primarily with the process of sanctification. Selected passages suggest the means by which this process is achieved. Each of these is conducive to evangelism.

(1) *Humility.*—This Paul sets forth as he says "to every man that is among you, not to think of himself more highly than he ought to think; but to think soberly, according as God hath dealt to every man the measure of faith" (Rom.

2. Ibid., p. 403.
3. The emphasis upon sanctification in this section is upon the outworkings of the fruits of the Spirit (cf. Gal. 5:22–26).

12:3). Since his own condition is a gift from God, there is no place for undue pride (cf. 1 Cor. 15:10; Eph. 3:8). Every Christian is a sinner saved by grace who should endeavor to share that grace with others.

Lack of humility can be fatal to an evangelist. He should never preach down to those whom he would win. Instead he should seek to identify himself with the sinner (John 17:15).

A hard and wicked man was awaiting execution. Many pastors had tried, without success, to win him to Christ. Each in turn talked to him about what a great sinner he was, and how he needed salvation. Their only effect was to harden his heart further. Finally a humble layman asked to see the man. He said, "You and I are in a terrible fix, aren't we?" Soon the man was in tears, as he repented of his sins and trusted in the Saviour.

(2) *Dedication.*—The very essence of sanctification is dedication. This involves every phase of one's being. In Romans 12:4-8 Paul returns to the figure of Christians as parts of the body of Christ. Listing gifts of the Holy Spirit such as prophecy, ministry, exhortation, giving, ruling (literally, the one standing in front), and the showing of mercy (vv. 4-8), he exhorts that these shall be used in the manner intended by the Holy Spirit. They are not to be the source of pride, but of diligent and spiritual application.

It is not how talented a person may be that matters. The important thing is how he uses his abilities. A woman criticized Dwight L. Moody's preaching because of his faulty grammar. He replied: "You seem to have grammar good enough. What are you doing with it for the Lord?" This is the supreme question for every Christian.

(3) *Co-operation.*—The sanctified person will practice co-operation with his brethren, rather than be a source of strife and disturbance. This Paul avows in Romans 12:9-10: "Let love be without dissimulation [hypocrisy]. . . . Be kindly affectioned one to another with brotherly love [in love of

the brethren]; in honour preferring one another." (Cf. 1 Cor. 12:14.)

Lack of co-operation is like pouring steel filings into the working parts of a delicate mechanism. A co-operative spirit is oil which insures its proper function. Strife among Christian people renders ineffective the work of evangelism more than any other one thing. The higher a person is in church leadership, the more Satan considers him a choice tool. A Christian is not to be a "yes" man. But there is no virtue in individuality for individuality's sake. God is not the author of confusion. A proud, self-seeking spirit has no place in his work. It takes more Christian virtue to serve as a member of a committee than to be its chairman. It is better still not to be on the committee at all, but to co-operate in its findings, provided they rest upon Christian principles.

On a businessman's desk was this motto in the form of a prayer: "God give me grace to serve without caring who gets the credit."

(4) *Optimism.*—"Rejoicing in hope" (Rom. 12:12), or in the sphere of hope, is Paul's way of expressing it. It is very easy for a Christian to become discouraged. This is true especially in the work of evangelism. In it one is dealing in intangibles, wherein progress is hard to be charted. Only as the evangel remembers that he is "serving the Lord" (v. 11), can he rejoice in hope. God never demands success, only faithfulness. But he promises victory to those who are faithful in his work.

A man introduced a visitor whom he had brought to Sunday school, saying that he had made thirty-five visits to the man. When asked why he made thirty-five, he replied, "Because thirty-four did not bring him."

(5) *Patience.*—Paul continues, "Patient in tribulation" (Rom. 12:12). This is a companion virtue to "rejoicing in hope." The word "patient" was used as a military citation for a soldier who stood up to the enemy's charge, and had enough in reserve to countercharge to victory. So in the

midst of tribulation the Christian is to find in the Holy Spirit reserve strength necessary to overcome all obstacles. This is further stated in verses 14 and 17-21. The Christian is to bless, and curse not. As far as possible he is to live peaceably with all men. He should never be overcome of evil, but should overcome evil with good. This he will do, if he is fervent in the realm of the Holy Spirit as he serves the Lord (Rom. 12:11).

In soul-winning one may receive abuse or passive resistance from the lost person. In either case his patience must be exercised. If evil men abuse him, they abused his Lord before him. Passive resistance will not be overcome by physical effort or by discouragement in the effort. But perserverance bathed in compassion will win the cause. A frozen river may be temporarily opened up with dynamite, only to freeze again. The silent, warm rays of the sun will turn it into a flowing stream.

During a revival meeting Dr. Charles E. Matthews and the pastor sat in a car one night with a lost man. Every kind of approach failed to move him. Finally the pastor began to weep over this lost soul. His compassionate tears melted the heart of the man, and soon he was saved. Here was patient endurance.

(6) *Prayer.*—Paul exhorted the Roman Christians to be "continuing instant in prayer" (Rom. 12:12). The evangel will not necessarily be constantly on his knees, though he must spend much time there. But his entire life must be lived in the attitude and atmosphere of prayer. This element has not been placed sixth because it is in that order of importance. The purpose is simply to follow Paul's own outline. Prayer must permeate and undergird every other element of sanctification.

Prayer is a prime requisite in soul-winning. And it must be continuous. After a young man had been saved in a service, a woman said: "I have prayed for this young man for years. At times I feared that I wearied the Lord with my prayers." Not so! For Jesus said "that men ought always to pray, and not to faint" (Luke 18:1; cf. Luke 18:2-8). The word "faint" was used of a soldier on a gruelling march falling out because of weariness.

Where it is possible prayer must have feet and legs to reach its maximum effectiveness. A humorous story is apropos. A man stood before the judge charged with stealing a turkey. He said that his crime was in answer to prayer. When asked to explain, he said: "I prayed for the Lord to send me a turkey. When nothing happened, I prayed for the Lord to send me after a turkey."

One may not agree with his theology, but he can learn from his philosophy. Christian people pray that souls will be saved. A more effective prayer is that the Lord will send them after souls (Luke 10:2).

(7) *Public relations and private example.*—These phases of Christian growth are dealt with in Romans 13:1-10 and 14:1-6, 21. A Christian should be a good citizen. Wherever he goes his presence should be charged with the power of the Holy Spirit. One man credited another with winning him to Christ. He said, "He never spoke to me of Christ, but he lived Christ before me." "Brother Bryan," a Presbyterian pastor, blessed the life of Birmingham as, perhaps, no other of its citizens. On one occasion a newspaper published his picture as hovering over the entire city. He was not a great pulpiteer. But wherever he went he was found praying for people. After his death grateful friends erected his statue, in the posture of prayer, in a conspicuous place in the city.

But a Christian is to exemplify Christ in his personal relations as well. A righteous man drove his children from the church because he practiced one attitude in church and another at home. Another man won a neighbor, with whom he was unacquainted, to Christ and to his church. It was accomplished, according to the neighbor, because Sunday after Sunday, in fair weather and foul, he observed the man going to Sunday school with his Bible under his arm.

The stronger a Christian becomes, the greater his responsibility for his weaker Christian brethren (Rom. 14:1-13). Censorious criticism must give place to Christian concern and understanding. Conduct which may be relatively harmless to the stranger, may prove to be a snare to the weaker person. The attitude of a truly sanctified Christian is expressed in Paul's words: "Wherefore, if meat make my brother to offend, I will eat no flesh while the world standeth, lest I make my brother to offend [stumble]" (1 Cor. 8:13).

3. *The Work of an Evangelist*

To Timothy, Paul wrote, "Do the work of an evangelist, make full proof of thy ministry" (2 Tim. 4:5). Loosely rendered this may well read, "Let every thing that you do be characterized by the work of an evangelist. Fill full your work as a servant of the Lord." This may well apply to every Christian.

The aforementioned elements of sanctification must not be made an end within themselves. Indeed, such an attitude will not achieve sanctification at all, but merely outward adornment for self-satisfaction and personal glory. The goodness of such a Christian can become pernicious evil so far as God's redemptive purpose is concerned.

Too much emphasis is placed upon the negative side of goodness. A man is said to be a good Christian if he does not follow evil practices. By this standard a mannequin would qualify. But all that it is good for is to model clothes.

To be used of the Holy Spirit in evangelism, a Christian must be positively good. And his goodness should be to the end that God will be glorified in souls won to Christ (Matt. 5:16).

III. Sanctification, an Ultimate Goal

The process of sanctification involves the entire life of the Christian and demands his every effort wrought in the power of the Holy Spirit. Sanctification will not be achieved in a moment. Like a child learning to walk, the Christian may stumble and fall. But he must rise to try again. With each such rising, he will become more proficient. As an exercise, take the aforementioned elements in sanctification and try them. They may prove difficult at first, but keep on trying. Efficient service for Christ will be the reward.

1. The End of Sanctification, Glorification

This goal is seen in Paul's words in Romans 8:30: "Moreover whom he did predestinate, them he also called: and whom he called, them he also justified: and whom he justified, them he also glorified." God predestinated a plan of salvation. He calls all men to receive it. Those who respond, he justifies. His purpose is to glorify those who have been declared just.

This purpose is expressed in Romans 8:29: ". . . to be conformed to the image of his Son, that he might be the first-born among many brethren." The word "conformed" means to be made in outward expression to coincide with one's inward nature. "Thus, in the process of sanctification, the saint is transformed in his inner heart life to resemble the Lord Jesus, which inner change results in the outward expression that reflects the beauty of the Lord Jesus." [4]

That this is a gradual growth is seen in Philippians 1:9-11. Paul prays "that your love may abound yet more and more in knowledge and in all judgment; that ye may approve things that are excellent; that ye may be sincere and without

4. Kenneth S. Wuest, *Romans in the Greek New Testament* (Grand Rapids: Eerdmans Publishing Company, 1955), p. 145.

offence till the day of Christ; being filled with the fruits of righteousness, which are by Jesus Christ, unto the glory and praise of God" (cf. Eph. 4:13).

The full realization of sanctification will be in "the day of Christ." Then, "when Christ, who is our life, shall appear, then shall ye also appear with him in glory" (Col. 3:4). "Beloved, now are we the sons of God, and it doth not yet appear what we shall be: but we know that, when he shall appear, we shall be like him; for we shall see him as he is" (1 John 3:2).

2. *The Degrees of Glorification*

Paradoxical though it may seem, the New Testament teaches degrees of glorification. In Romans 14:10-12 Paul says that every Christian shall stand before the judgment seat of Christ to give account of himself to God. This judgment will not be with respect to redemption but to rewards. And these rewards will be in proportion to our service to Christ through our ministry to others (Matt. 25:34-40).

Each child of God will enjoy heaven to the full extent of his capacity, said capacity being in direct proportion to the degree of his sanctification in this present life. Two men hear a symphony orchestra with full enjoyment. But one's enjoyment is greater because he goes to the concert with a musical development which enhances his ability to appreciate the concert.

The truth taught by Jesus in the parable of the unjust steward is that each person should use his present opportunities in such manner that when he arrives in heaven he will be welcomed by those who are there because of his work while on earth (Luke 16:1-9). Obviously his glory or joy will exceed that of the man who fails in this stewardship and whose arrival in heaven receives no such welcome. This is a thought for all Christians to ponder while opportunity in evangelism remains.

3. *The Means to Complete Glorification*

This is expressed in Romans 8:14-18: "For as many as are led by the Spirit of God, they are the sons of God. . . . And if children, then heirs; heirs of God, and joint-heirs with Christ; if so be that we suffer with him, that we may be also glorified together. For I reckon that the sufferings of this present time are not worthy to be compared with the glory which shall be revealed in us." One must suffer with Christ if he expects to be fully glorified with him.

At the conclusion of a hard-fought and victorious football game, there are joy and glory among the spectators. But the greater joy and glory fall upon those who fought, suffered, and won on the field of battle. In this finite illustration there is the suggestion of infinite truth.

4. *The Present Responsibility*

In the midst of a changing and uncertain world Peter asks, "What manner of persons ought ye to be?" (2 Peter 3:11). As though in answer, Paul says, "Walk in wisdom toward them that are without [lost people], redeeming the time" (Col. 4:5). "Redeeming the time" means to go into the market place and buy up the time. Christian people should walk wisely in the proper use of time, in order to win lost people to Christ.

This calls for a sense of awareness. "Knowing the time, that now it is high time to awake out of sleep" (Rom. 13:11). "To awake," in the original language, expresses an urgent action to be done by another. That critical period in history should awake them from the sleep induced by complacency and sinful living.

Such an awareness should result in righteous and positive living. Paul continues, "The night is far spent, the day is at hand: let us therefore cast off the works of darkness, and let us put on the armour of light" (Rom. 13:12). Verse 13 details these works of darkness, and verse 14 suggests the armor of light. In short, Paul says, "Put off your sleeping, or night clothes, and put on your fighting, or day clothes." This latter suggests not merely abstaining from evil, but positive action in that which is good.

Evangelism is Christian warfare. Napoleon said that conquest made him and must sustain him. This is true of the cause of Christ (cf. Heb. 2:10; 2 Tim. 2:3-4). For a Christian to be a "good soldier of Jesus Christ" three things are necessary.

(1) *Put on the Lord Jesus.*—A Christian must "Put . . . on the Lord Jesus Christ" (Rom. 13:14). Christ is the garment which every Christian must wear. Putting on Christ the Christian clothes himself in the moral practices and spiritual attitudes which are found in Christ. A missionary asked Gandhi what Christianity could do to win India. He replied, "Let the Christians live like Jesus Christ."

(2) *Be endued with power.*—A Christian must "be endued with power from on high" (Luke 24:49). Literally, "Get yourselves clothed with power from on high." This is the power of the Holy Spirit. And in so doing, the Lord's people are to begin where they are and evangelize the whole world (Luke 24:47-49; Acts 1:8).

The Christian is indwelt by the Holy Spirit. He gets himself clothed with the Spirit's power through positive righteousness, Bible study, prayer, and complete dedication of his powers to God through Christ (cf. Rom. 6:13).

At the outset of World War II young men by the millions were brought into training camps. After they had learned military science and tactics, they were sent into combat. There they suffered. Many died. But history records their heroic deeds and victory. It is no wonder that Paul was so fond of military terms in expressing Christian truth.

(3) *Do the Lord's work.*—"Be . . . in the work of the Lord" (1 Cor. 15:58). What is the work of the Lord? Recall chapter

5. This is the work of the Lord. His people must be in the work of the Lord. They can do so with the assurance of victory, "forasmuch as ye know that your labour is not in vain in the Lord" (1 Cor. 15:58).

FOR DISCUSSION AND CLASSWORK

1. What is the difference between sanctification as taught by Baptists and certain holiness groups?
2. Is sanctification instantaneous, a process, or both?
3. Should a Christian seek to destroy his body or dedicate it to God? What are some ways to dedicate the body?
4. Is it possible for a true Christian to be one thing at home and another at church?
5. Let the class members describe the best Christian each one knows.

Suggestions to the Teacher

CHAPTER 1

1. Read the article on "Evangelism" in the *Encyclopedia of Southern Baptists*.
2. For modern methods of writing in evangelism examine various publications of the Baptist Sunday School Board, Nashville, Tennessee.
3. Read two volumes by Charles E. Matthews, *The Southern Baptist Program of Evangelism* (Home Mission Board), and *Every Christian's Job* (Convention Press).

CHAPTER 2

1. Using a Bible concordance, study passages dealing with sin, blood, salvation, and judgment.
2. On sin, salvation, atonement, and election read chapters on these in *Fundamentals of Our Faith*, by Herschel H. Hobbs (Broadman Press).

CHAPTER 3

1. Read the chapter on "Holy Spirit" in *Fundamentals of Our Faith*.
2. Read Acts and check the references on the Holy Spirit with John 14 to 16.

CHAPTER 4

1. Read articles on "Grace" in *Encyclopedia of Southern Baptists*, *The International Standard Bible Encyclopaedia*, and Hastings' *Dictionary of the Bible*.
2. Read *Ephesians: Pattern for Christian Living*, by Ray Summers (Broadman Press).

CHAPTER 5

1. Read *Evangelism According to Christ*, by G. S. Dobbins (Broadman Press), and *With Christ After the Lost*, by L. R. Scarborough (Broadman Press).

CHAPTER 6

1. At one sitting read Romans to determine the contents of the gospel.
2. Read *The Book of Acts,* by Frank Stagg (Broadman Press).

CHAPTER 7

1. See articles on religious education in the *Encyclopedia of Southern Baptists.*
2. An exhaustive study may be found in *Introduction to Religious Education,* by Price, Carpenter, and Chapman (Macmillan).

CHAPTER 8

1. Check articles on "Saint" and "Sanctification" in *Encyclopedia of Southern Baptists* and Hastings' *Dictionary of the Bible.*
2. For a study of Hebrews as a call to world missions see *Studies in Hebrews,* by Herschel H. Hobbs (Convention Press).

Suggested Audio-Visual Aids
for Teaching This Book

THE USE OF a chalkboard throughout the teaching of this book is recommended. If a chalkboard is not available, butcher paper or other low cost paper can be mounted on a table turned on its end.

A flip chart is suggested also. If you cannot obtain or make a flip chart, you may substitute posters or the chalkboard.

CHAPTER 1

FLIP CHART: Use the word *euaggelizo* and show its meaning as a verb, noun, and title.

CHALKBOARD: Place the words, "preach," "teach," "disciple," and "write" on a chalkboard and cover them with strips of paper in such a way that they can be revealed as you discuss them.

SLIDE: Show a slide of a baby (a frame from one of the Nursery filmstrips will do).

FILMSTRIP: *Witness to the World,* 46 frames; color; with manual. (26b) $5.00; recording $2.00.

MOTION PICTURE: *Salvation and Christian Fellowship,* 16 minutes; rental, black and white, $6.00; color, $9.00.

SENTENCE STRIPS: Make sentence strips of the Scripture verses used in the chapter. Place them on a sentence strip board.

CHAPTER 2

CHALKBOARD: Draw two parallel lines to explain the word "infinite."

FLIP CHART: Draw a diagram to illustrate the two covenants mentioned in the chapter.

FILMSTRIP: *Ye Are Witnesses,* 36 frames; with captions and manual. (26b) $3.00. Additional manuals 10¢ per copy.

MOTION PICTURE: *A Faithful Witness,* 14 minutes; rental, black and white, $6.00; color, $9.00.

CHAPTER 3

FLIP CHART: Draw a diagram showing how a dam can force the flow of a river through a turbine.

FILMSTRIPS: *Witness to an Ethiopian,* 40 frames; color; with manual. (26b) $5.00; recording, $2.00.

A Lost Soldier, 44 frames; color; with manual. (26b) $5.00; recording, $2.00.

MOTION PICTURE: *Endued with Power,* 18 minutes; rental, black and white, $6.00; color, $9.00.

OPAQUE: Obtain a picture showing a surgeon operating. Mount and project.

FLIP CHART: Put the two words "comforter" and "paraclete" and show the meaning of each one.

CHAPTER 4

FLIP CHART: Show how many times Paul used the word "gift." Show how many times the word "grace" was used in the New Testament and compare with how many times Paul used it.

CHALKBOARD: Write the words "ecumenical movement" and let the class members suggest meanings of the movement.

CHAPTER 5

FLIP CHART: Illustrate the depraved nature of man.

SLIDE: A 350 *Sanyati—Baptist Hospital;* Pastor Sitole witnessing to a patient. Slide available from the Division of Visual Education, Foreign Mission Board, Richmond, Virginia; 25¢ each.

CHALKBOARD: List the methods of teaching; show how different methods, (such as visual aids) may be combined.

CHAPTER 6

MOTION PICTURE: *Endued with Power,* 18 minutes; rental, black and white, $6.00; color, $9.00.

FILMSTRIP: *A Lost City,* 39 frames; color; with manual. (26b) $5.00; recording, $2.00.

FLIP CHART: Draw a chart of the churches in the association showing their membership and the number of conversions (a number of charts could be used here in conjunction with an interview with the superintendent of missions).

CHAPTER 7

OBJECTS: Obtain a model church and a globe and prepare an interest center to show what religious education must teach our people.

POSTER: Illustrate by cartoon or diagram the Training Union's part in religious education and soul-winning.

MOTION PICTURE: *How to Visit,* 13 minutes; rental, $4.00.
FLIP CHART: List the religious education activities in your church.

CHAPTER 8

FILMSTRIP: *This They Believed,* 42 frames; color; with manual.
(26b) $5.00; recording, $2.00.
MOTION PICTURE: *Every Christian a Missionary,* 14 minutes;
rental, black and white, $6.00; color, $9.00.

Questions for Review and Written Work

For instructions concerning the written work and the requesting of awards, see "Requirements for Credit in Class or Home Study," page ix.

Chapter 1

1. Why is the New Testament the only rule of faith and practice for New Testament churches? What is the relation between the Old and New testaments?
2. What is the meaning of the word "evangelism"?
3. In what three ways is the word "salvation" used in the New Testament?
4. What are the five elements in New Testament evangelism?

Chapter 2

5. What is meant by the divine will?
6. In what way is the crucifixion related to eternity?
7. Name the six elements involved in Jesus' redemptive work.
8. What is involved in the doctrine of "election"?

Chapter 3

9. How is the Holy Spirit related to the Trinity?
10. In what ways does the Holy Spirit work in winning the lost?
11. What is the sin against the Holy Spirit?
12. What are some of the gifts of the Holy Spirit? What is the meaning of "tongues"?

Chapter 4

13. Who are the involved personalities in evangelism?
14. What is the obligation placed upon the Christian?
15. Name two results of neglecting this obligation.
16. What are the consequences involved in this neglect?

CHAPTER 5

17. What are the moral attributes of God?
18. Why cannot man be saved by keeping the law of Moses?
19. Where did Jesus place the primary emphasis in his ministry? Why?
20. In what ways did Jesus seek the lost?

CHAPTER 6

21. What are the five principles assumed by first-century Christians in evangelism?
22. Discuss briefly the program of evangelism followed by New Testament Christians.
23. What scriptural support is there for emphasizing results in evangelism?

CHAPTER 7

24. Define religious education. Why is it synonymous with evangelism?
25. What are the various phases of religious education?
26. What are the methods employed in Sunday school evangelism?
27. What is the goal of New Testament evangelism? What organization is primarily responsible for reaching this goal?

CHAPTER 8

28. What are the four elements involved in the instantaneous experience of sanctification?
29. Why is sanctification also a continuing process?
30. What is the ultimate goal of sanctification?
31. What is meant by degrees of glorification?